The Road to Repentance

A Televangelist's Story:
From Ruin to Restoration

The Road to Repentance

A Televangelist's Story:
From Ruin to Restoration

Marvin E. Gorman

1440 State Hwy 248 Suite Q-167
Branson, MO 65616
www.marvingorman.com
417-336-4685

ISBN 1-931600-91-0

Dedication

To my devoted and faithful wife, Virginia, who has walked with me through the deepest valleys and highest mountains of my life.

To Randy, Mark, Beverly, their spouses, and our eight grandchildren, whose love and support exceed what any father could ask.

To the relatives on both sides of our family, my wife's and mine, who stood by us without wavering.

Just prior to this book going to press, the Lord promoted my dear mother-in-law to Glory. During the darkest days of my life, following the exposure of my fall, no person was more loyal and dedicated in supporting me than she was. Her love, confidence in me, and commitment to my total restoration never wavered.

Acknowledgments

Because of the commitment, sacrificial efforts, and contributions of my lovely wife, Virginia, as well as of the following people, this book has become a reality: Richard and Sandy Gazowsky; John Avanzini; Neil Eskelin; Mary Helen Bryant; Svein Hamre; Sherwood Jansen; Juanita Aranda; and Wayne and Cheryl Jones.

Endorsement

I feel that the spirit of the author of this book is honest and clean, and that this book can be of real value to the Body of Christ as they see a living example of true repentance, true redemption, and full restoration beyond what our religious dogma has allowed.

Dr. Fuchsia T. Pickett

Contents

Foreword

It would be easy to be highly critical about what happened between Marvin Gorman and Jimmy Swaggart. However, both of these great men are choice servants of the Most High God, and are greatly loved by Him. Sometimes we forget that the tragedies that befall ministers of the gospel are more than events that merely involve buildings, non-profit organizations, and television programs. These ministers are flesh-and-blood individuals who suffer as much, or more, than anyone else when these catastrophes happen. Neither Marvin nor Jimmy went into the ministry of the gospel of Jesus Christ with the intention of doing anything other than giving their lives for their precious Lord and Savior. However, many times events and situations draw the man or woman of God ever so slowly away from the God-given calling and purpose.

I never think of those who have disappointed God without thinking of the little widow woman at Zarephath. Regretfully, she is primarily remembered for her worst day, not her best. First Kings 17 tells us of a day when God spoke audibly with her and told her to feed His prophet. Most people give no attention to those days; they only focus on the day she refused to obey God's command. However, that was not the end of her story. The best part of her life came when she changed her mind and fed Elijah throughout the duration of the drought. The best part of the story is her turnaround when she repented and rededicated her life to the task that God had given her.

This book is proof that this same great process of restoration and inner healing is working in the life of Marvin Gorman. I have personally read this manuscript at least six times. Each time I went through it, I listened closely to hear the voice of self-justification coming forth. I never once heard even a whimper of blame-placing on anyone except himself. In this book I hear a man of God who has greatly offended his Savior, and knows it. It tells of a man who seeks and obtains God's forgiveness and a new nod of approval. In this book, I hear a heartfelt desire from Marvin that all would be well with Jimmy Swaggart and his family. Now, this may not have always been the case. However, what's important is how Marvin Gorman feels about things *now*. Thank God, I can say he is on the mend, preaching the gospel of Jesus Christ, and looking for opportunities to make things right with everyone he has hurt.

In *The Road to Repentance*, Marvin deals primarily with what he has learned and how he can use it to help hurting people overcome their pain. Not only does he want to help the people he has hurt, but anyone else who has felt the pain of inner wounding. Great healing lies between the covers of this book. It can bring healing to you, even if you don't consciously realize you were hurt.

I close this foreword with an anonymous saying that has always spoken to me of the truly repentant offender: "The bird with the broken wing may never fly as high. But oh! How sweet is his new song!"

This book records the sweet song of a truly repentant servant of the Most High God.

John Avanzini, President
International FaithCenter\
HIS Image Ministries

Introduction

When I was handed the wafer-thin airmail envelope, my heart sank. I didn't want to open it. The letter was from Rodney, a missionary in the Middle East.

As I stood motionless in my office, my mind flashed back to when he was just eight years old. I could see young Rodney praying at a camp meeting altar, worshiping God with a pure, innocent heart. His family and ours had been close friends for years.

I remembered the days he came to our house for his weekly piano lesson from my wife, Virginia. It was during those formative years that God placed an unmistakable call on his life to become a missionary.

Later, when I became the pastor of the First Assembly of God in New Orleans, Louisiana, I was thrilled beyond words to financially support Rodney and his family as they entered one of the toughest mission fields in the world, the Middle East.

His task was not an easy one, for he ministered on the dusty streets of a predominantly Muslim country. He was under constant fear of reprisals from a totalitarian government.

Why did I hesitate to open the letter? Because I knew why Rodney was writing.

At that time the opening shots had already been fired in a conflict that resulted in the fall of three major television ministries: First, Marvin Gorman Ministries, then Jim Bakker's PTL Club, and finally the Jimmy Swaggart Evangelistic Association. The events surrounding the battle shook the evangelical world to its core.

The news of the incredible accusations made by Jimmy Swaggart against me were not confined to New Orleans or Baton Rouge, Louisiana. They were emblazoned on the pages of *USA Today* and became Ted Koppel's topic on ABC's *Nightline*. The major wire services carried the stories to the far corners of the world.

Some government and religious leaders in foreign lands were making a public mockery of Christianity. Rodney was caught in the crossfire and I was sick inside.

The disturbing events in America were offered as proof that Christianity was not real. Many of the newly converted Arab Christians were shaken and disillusioned. Now, with tearstained faces, they were questioning Rodney.

I could almost hear them as they asked, "If Jesus is so wonderful, why would His ministers fight each other?"

After reading Rodney's letter, I placed it on my desk and stared blankly at the books that lined the walls of my office. I had failed my friend. I cried out, "Lord, how could all of this happen? When will this terrible ordeal end?"

Each highly visible ministry was rocked by the revelation of an internal problem. All three ministers involved had been ordained by the world's largest Pentecostal denomination, the Assemblies of God.

The outfall was devastating. The denomination dealt severely with each of the ministers, but the problem became much more widespread. It was the hot topic of discussion in neighborhood barber shops and was constant fodder for the joke writers of the late-night talk shows. By the end of 1988, nearly every Christian in the world had been affected in some manner by these events.

I cringed when I heard the story of a man by the name of Dean who was a tattoo artist in San Francisco's Broadway district. He was trained under the famous

Tuttle, a well-known tattoo artist of the 1960's. Dean had been tattooed on every part of his body, excluding his face, hands, and feet. When he became a born-again Christian, he took a sledge hammer to his Broadway shop, literally smashing his equipment into oblivion. He declared, "I am burning my bridges so I can never walk this way again."

Dean quickly found employment in a San Francisco print shop. The testimony of his conversion was well received by his boss and those who worked with him. He remembered the joy he felt as he walked past the office of his employer and saw him wiping tears from his eyes as he watched a Jimmy Swaggart telecast.

However, all this was about to change. When the televangelists fell, Dean became the object of open ridicule. His Christian witness had been more than neutralized. It had been obliterated.

The results still linger. Recently, the Gallup poll organization asked Americans to identify the "least trusted" professions. A score of 1 was the most trusted and a score of 50 was the least. At the bottom of the poll, sandwiched between the last place Mafia (50) and used-car salesmen (48), were the televangelists. They ranked an embarrassing number 49.

Why have I written this book? It is for Rodney. It is for Dean. It is for the countless people who have suffered an anguish and embarrassment that cannot be fully described. It is my prayerful desire to see the hurt, despair, and frustration that came to the Church in the late 1980's wiped away. I believe the time has come to close the door on these tragic events.

I am writing these words to bring restoration, healing, and shining rays of hope to the dark corners of Christianity—to the places where many Christians still hide because of the ridicule and scorn they have suffered.

God used my clash with Jimmy Swaggart to help me discover the root causes of my own crushing failure and to bring me closer to Him than I ever dreamed possible. The Lord has shown me how He can bring inner healing to those who are living in fear, troubled by the thought of the exposure of a past or continuing sin.

It is not my purpose to dwell on past mistakes that have been reported in the press and embellished in the tabloids. They are presented only as a prelude to the *real* story how the Lord corrects His leadership and restores lives. Waiting ahead is not only hope, but a glorious future!

Chapter 1

The Moment of Truth

On a sun-drenched Louisiana afternoon I turned the wheel of my car into the parking lot of a seedy motel on Airline Highway, on the outskirts of New Orleans. If I live to be a hundred, I will never forget the date: October 17, 1987.

I veered my vehicle next to the yellow Lincoln where a man was kneeling. He was changing the right front tire. In the background I could hear, through the partially opened doors of unoccupied rooms, televisions blaring an unending barrage of explicit, adult videos.

It was obvious that the motel had known days of greater fortune. Now the swimming pool was filled with dirt and weeds. The withered grass growing underneath the phantom diving board gave an eerie, haunting atmosphere to the place.

I was nervous and my heart was in my throat. The man whom I was about to talk to had once been my friend. His mother had been like a mother to me. I remembered a phone call I received from her early the morning she passed away to give *me* words of encouragement. What a great woman she was!

Now I was about to confront her son, a man who was bigger than life to the millions of people who watched him on television every week. Just ahead of me was Jimmy Swaggart.

I knew Jimmy was at the motel with a prostitute because friends had informed me. At that moment my thoughts turned to the words the Lord had spoken to me as I drove to this pivotal encounter: "Be careful how you judge Jimmy, for with the same judgment that you judge him, you shall also be judged."

With that reminder still echoing in my thoughts, I opened the car door and walked toward Jimmy. He was kneeling, re-installing a tire that I later learned he had nervously bolted on backwards. He quickly explained, "I had a flat tire and I needed to change it."

"Jimmy," I responded, "you are not here because of a flat tire. I know the real reason. My friend cut your tire stem so that you would be delayed and I could drive here to talk with you. Let's go to the trunk and look at your tire."

We walked to the back of his car. When he opened the trunk we both stared at the severed air stem. I glanced at Jimmy and saw his rigid, defensive posture melt away like butter.

When I saw his manner, my thoughts immediately turned to a happier time several years earlier when Jimmy and I were much closer friends. It was in St. Louis, Missouri, at an international convention of the Assemblies of God. I happened to be near the registration desk at the headquarters hotel while Jimmy was checking in. To his surprise, reservations had been made for all of his 25 or so staff members, but someone had inadvertently forgotten to reserve a room for Jimmy. Instead of pounding on the desk and demanding a room, his response was one of humility. He simply asked, "Could you see if it is possible to work something out?" He then quietly walked over to a seat in the lobby and waited patiently for the solution to his dilemma.

An Ominous Cloud

There is a great deal of history that led to our uncomfortable meeting at that disreputable motel.

Nine years earlier, in 1978, I made a tragic mistake. I turned my back on principles that had been the guiding force of my life. I committed an act of adultery.

A minister's wife, whom I was counseling, called my office and led me to believe that her emotional situation was so desperate that she was contemplating suicide. I foolishly abandoned my ministerial protocol and hurriedly went by myself to her hotel room.

That transgression became a dark, ominous cloud hanging over my life and ministry. During the months and years that followed, I repented daily. Only the Lord knows the tears I shed. Yet there was a heavy haze of fear that hovered over me like a menacing giant.

At this same time, through God's grace, my ministry was experiencing its greatest days of success and blessing. Our church in New Orleans, First Assembly of God, had grown to 6,000. We had five services each Sunday and a Monday evening miracle rally in order to accommodate the people in our 1200-seat auditorium.

Our daily television ministry included a live program on which I answered questions from callers from around the nation. We were also in the process of purchasing two television stations. A few years earlier I had been elected to serve on the 13-member Executive Board of the Assemblies of God denomination.

In 1985, because of the growth, our church in New Orleans entered into an ambitious building program and the new sanctuary was nearing completion. We were just six months away from worshiping in the new facility.

My Greatest Fear

At what seemed like the apex of my ministry I received a phone call at my office that would change my life forever. It was July 15, 1986. "Marvin, do you have time for me to stop by and see you today?" the minister asked.

Over the years the caller had met with me on several occasions on a variety of topics, but this seemed urgent. "Sure," I told him, "but the earliest I can see you is at four o'clock this afternoon."

He was on time.

Just a few seconds after he closed the door the man spoke words I never expected to hear. He looked at me and said, "We know about you and my wife."

My greatest fear became a shocking reality. Seated before me was the husband of the woman with whom I had the failure many years earlier.

I asked, "You know what?"

He replied, "Brother Gorman, she told me that she confessed everything to another minister and right now he is waiting for a phone call from you."

Then the concerned man said, "I'm so sorry she felt it necessary to bring someone else into this. If she had only told me, I know the three of us could have worked this thing out."

Immediately I called the minister and arranged for a meeting with him, the husband, and me.

I didn't realize what I was walking into. The meeting was a disaster. Whether because of jealousy, anger, or indignation, the pastor showed little compassion and railed against me without mercy. The minister threatened that if I didn't go to Jimmy Swaggart immediately, he would call my family and the members of my board.

The husband of the woman involved passively watched the proceedings.

I commented, "I don't know where Jimmy is. Besides, I believe this is a matter that should be taken to the District Superintendent of the denomination."

"I don't trust the Superintendent," the pastor countered. "I think Jimmy Swaggart is the only man who can handle it."

"I'm not sure I can get in touch with him," I repeated.

Without a pause he said, "I can get hold of him in three minutes."

The moment he spoke those words, I knew I had been lured into a trap. I later learned that Jimmy knew everything that was going on and was waiting for the call.

Out of Time

My mind was reeling. I wanted to do something to stop the chain of events I saw unfolding. I needed time to confess to my family, time to resign from my church.

There wasn't time. With one phone call I was forced into an immediate meeting with Jimmy in Baton

Rouge, about 80 miles west of New Orleans. I assumed there would be four people present: the three of us who had just met, plus Jimmy.

When I arrived at his office, I was shocked to see his attorney and the senior minister on his staff.

I will never forget the scene. I was seated on one side of the table and the rest of the group faced me. For two and a half hours, Jimmy Swaggart's voice rose with anger. He was not only accusing me of sin with the wife of the man who was present, but of "multiple liaisons" with several other women. Later, as the rumors became more exaggerated, that number increased to approximately a hundred women. I was so shocked I hardly knew how to respond.

When there was a pause in the conversation I answered, "Yes, Jimmy, I sinned in 1978 but it is nothing like what you are saying."

Finally, after I had been severely chastised to the point of exhaustion, Jimmy walked over to his desk and picked up a Bible. It was already opened to the Book of First Timothy. He began to read the apostle Paul's admonition: "Against an elder receive not an accusation, but before two or three witnesses. Them that sin rebuke before all, that others also may fear" (1 Tim. 5:19-20).

My understanding of that Scripture is that the offender is to be rebuked before the rest of the elders, not before an entire congregation that includes new Christians.

The interpretation of this group, however, was totally different. They believed the whole world should know about my transgression. That's exactly what happened.

An Explosive Story

By the time I returned to New Orleans a few hours later, the story of the truth of my transgression, with many unfounded rumors added, was spreading through my church like wildfire.

Fortunately, no one had called my wife. The moment I reached our home, I tearfully revealed the matter to her. As I will discuss later, we were a broken, shattered couple.

In the days that followed, my staff, the board members of my church, and my congregation were falsely led to believe that there were signed statements by many women charging me with adultery. I was not given the privilege of appearing personally before the congregation. Confusion, anger, and emotional pain were running rampant.

My children were told that I had deceived them. The ultimatum given them was to turn against their father in order to remain part of the church. They made the decision to forgive me and to maintain unity in our family.

I was aghast at the allegations printed and circulated against me. The truth was mixed with untruth and the results were highly explosive. One letter in particular, alleging an extremely large number of sexual liaisons with different women, was mailed by the Swaggart organization to church leaders across the country and to many foreign nations.

The results were devastating. Suddenly, everything I had worked for came crashing down at lightning speed. My national television ministry collapsed and I was left with nearly seven million dollars of unpaid debts; unwillingly, I filed for bankruptcy.

What other punishment was in store?

Chapter 2

"What Do You Want?"

For eight agonizing months from the latter part of 1986 until early 1987, I did everything within my power to clear my tarnished name. With my wife by my side, I pleaded with the district officials of my denomination to forgive me for my transgression. "Please," I begged them, "tell me the names of my accusers."

"You'll have to work things out with Jimmy Swaggart," I was told, but the evangelist and his staff would not communicate with me on the topic and the accusations continued to circulate.

In March, 1987, I began receiving calls from the news department of Channel 4, a network affiliate in our city. They had assigned their top investigative reporter to prepare a television special concerning "the facts" of my story. In their attempt to interview me for the broadcast, a producer said, "Reverend, this program is going to destroy you. It contains horrible things and you need to refute them on camera."

"No," I replied. "I don't want to get into media bashing."

They were relentless. Since this was just a few days after the PTL scandal broke, it was a hot issue. The program was scheduled to air April 5, 1987. My picture was on the front cover of *TV Guide* and the special report was being promoted in the newspaper. The station saw a golden opportunity to garner some prime time ratings.

I did not know it at the time, but it was later revealed to me that the entire program had been orchestrated by Jimmy Swaggart's attorney.

Pleading My Case

The last week of March I filed a lawsuit against Jimmy Swaggart, his ministry, and other parties for the damage caused by unfounded rumors. I took legal action for two reasons. First, I desperately wanted to clear my name. Second, I hoped my action would cause the television station to cancel the scheduled program.

As a minister I was fully aware of what the Scriptures say about suing a brother. Then one day in prayer, the Lord clearly spoke to me concerning something in the

Word that related to my dilemma. He said, "Paul appealed to Caesar."

Immediately I began to read Acts, chapters 24, 25, and 26. When the apostle knew he could not get a fair hearing before the religious leaders, the Sanhedrin, he appealed directly to the courts of the land. He requested that his plea be made directly to Caesar (see Acts 25:11).

I felt I was in the same predicament. I had already attempted to present my case to church officials and had been refused.

I did not realize it at the time, but the lawsuit became tied to my bankruptcy. If successful, the court would be allowed to seize the assets of a settlement to clear the outstanding debts of Marvin Gorman Ministries.

Suddenly I began to feel like I was a modern-day Jonah in the belly of a legal nightmare. My future and the future of the lawsuit was out of my control. However, as I discovered, God used this detour for a purpose I did not understand.

The suit made headlines and the television special ran as scheduled.

Back at the Motel

The summer of 1987 was one of intense pressure. The Lord was blessing the new church we had started, yet we could not escape the attention of the media, the strain of finances, or the tension that continued between Jimmy Swaggart and me.

In the fall of that year, acting on information we had received, two men I hired drove to the unkempt motel on Airline Highway and documented the fact that the evangelist was in the company of a prostitute.

That is when I drove to the location and confronted him.

Jimmy and I both felt uncomfortable with the surroundings of the motel. "Marvin, we need to talk," he said as he finished changing the tire.

We drove our cars to a nearby parking lot and he walked over to sit in the front seat of my automobile. Immediately, he began to unburden his heart. Again and again in our lengthy conversation Jimmy expressed his greatest fear that God would take His Holy Spirit from him.

I felt Jimmy understood that it was not my desire to expose him, but to somehow bring the conflict in our situation to a point of healing. I said, "Jimmy, I am willing to meet with you once every week so we can pray together until you have victory."

Finally, in response to his request, I told him I would travel to Baton Rouge to be with him as he disclosed the circumstances to his wife, Frances. I followed him as we drove west. A few minutes later, he pulled to the shoulder of the road. As I stopped my car beside him, he came to me and said, "Marvin, I think it would be better if I told her myself." I left Jimmy as he headed for Baton Rouge and I drove home.

The next day Frances called me to arrange an immediate meeting. I agreed. That same afternoon I met with Jimmy, Frances, and their son Donnie. At the insistence of my family, I was accompanied by an attorney friend of mine.

The meeting, which lasted nearly four hours, was about much more than the motel incident. Jimmy kept asking, "Marvin, what do you want? What can I do for you?"

I responded, "Jimmy, I don't want anything but for you to be my friend and for you to get your life straightened out."

Both Jimmy and Frances continued to press: "Marvin, what are you going to do?"

Promises, Promises

During the following week Jimmy called me several times. He insisted that I bring my family to their home in Baton Rouge on Friday night, October 23, 1987. My wife, our two sons, and our son-in-law accompanied me for the six-hour meeting.

At one point I handed Jimmy a letter he had written and mailed to church officials and foreign missionaries alleging numerous infidelities. He admitted, "Marvin, I can't prove any of that." Then he added, "This is what caused the district church officials to be so hard on you. It is my fault you were driven into bankruptcy."

That evening Jimmy asked me what he could do to help with my situation. He offered jobs to me and my family. He strongly suggested that I close my newly established church in New Orleans and move to Baton Rouge to work with him.

"Jimmy," I told him, "I do not feel a release from my burden for the New Orleans area." In obedience to the Lord I knew I must continue my pastorate.

I had heard rumors that Jimmy was considering leaving his denomination and pulling hundreds of pastors with him. I told him, "Jimmy, if I see that you are planning to leave the Assemblies of God, I will not keep silent. I'm afraid that if you leave the denomination and your failings become known, you will lash out and cause more destruction."

At that time Jimmy knew there were two men who would testify that they had been at the motel in a room near the one he had used. He did not know there was also photographic evidence.

Jimmy volunteered to make a public apology on his television program and in his magazine for the injustices done to me, to my family, and to other ministers he had been lashing out against for a variety of reasons.

Four months went by with no word from him. In early February of 1988, I concluded that my attempts to help the situation were not effective. Earlier I had told Jimmy, "The information I have will not be used or released to anyone if you will just get your life in order and follow through on your promise to correct what you have done to me and to other ministers."

This did not happen.

A Tearful Confession

In late December of 1987, I learned that Jimmy was indeed making concrete plans to leave the Assemblies of God and form his own organization. It was one of the topics I had discussed with him in October, and was something I did not want to see take place because of the harm it would cause the denomination. I was no longer a minister of the Assemblies of God, but I continued to love the fellowship deeply.

I sent a letter to Jimmy, hand-delivered to him by one of our church staff. I wrote, "I see that you are not a man of your word...I am praying for God's direction as we look for other avenues that may be used."

I sought counsel from four godly men who advised me to meet with denominational officials.

It was not a hasty decision. I carefully studied what Jesus had to say about the situation I faced. Christ stated:

"Moreover if thy brother shall trespass against thee, go and tell him his fault between thee and him alone: if he shall hear thee, thou hast gained thy brother. But if he will not hear thee, then take with thee one or two more, that in the mouth of two or three witnesses every word may be established. And if he shall neglect to hear them, tell it unto the church..." (Matthew 18:15-17).

I had confronted Jimmy alone at the motel. Six days later, my wife, sons, and son-in-law accompanied me in a meeting with him. Now, we would take it to the leaders of the church.

On February 16, 1988, I flew to Springfield, Missouri, to meet at a hotel with the executives of the Assemblies of God denomination. I delivered to them the secret photographs that had been taken when I met Jimmy at the motel.

Reverend G. Raymond Carlson, General Superintendent, gave me a signed letter which stated:

"Dear Brother Gorman: Enclosed is the statement I have signed regarding the pictures which you shared with us at the Sheraton Hotel. The pictures and the statement will be kept under lock and key."

Four days after the meeting in Springfield, I flew to New York City to fulfill a speaking engagement at a Full Gospel church. I was shocked to find a host of newsmen waiting at my hotel to elicit some sort of statement from me concerning photos of Jimmy Swaggart with a woman at a motel. When I finally made my way to my room, refusing to give any information to the reporters, I was astounded to hear Ted Koppel calling from ABC's *Nightline* television program. Again, I refused to comment. I did not make the photos public and I do not know who did.

In 1991, four years after my lawsuit against Jimmy was filed, a jury was called and the case was tried before a judge. Day after day, for ten long weeks, Jimmy and Frances Swaggart were on one side of the courtroom and my wife and I were on the other.

What was the jury's decision? As you will learn, it was secondary to the great lessons the Lord taught me in this long and painful process.

There were times I wondered, "Will the wounds ever heal? Will life be meaningful again?"

Chapter 3

An Enemy Called Fear

Recently I was asked, "Marvin, in the years before your transgression came to light, what was it that most troubled you?"

The answer to that question was easy. "Fear," I told the questioner. "I lived in constant fear."

I had dealt with the issues of guilt and remorse and had experienced God's forgiveness. But until the source of my problem was brought to the surface, I continued to feel the crippling constrictions of fear.

I remember sitting in the den of my home located in a beautiful neighborhood of Metairie, a suburb of New Orleans. The memory of my liaison hung precariously over my life. On several occasions the woman threatened to destroy my ministry. Whenever she called, it was like someone was twisting a dagger into my heart.

The thought of losing my thriving church, my beautiful home, and my material possessions were not the only fears that plagued my mind. I worried most about losing my family if the truth was revealed, and the repercussions that would befall them.

One day, before the public revelation of my sin, I sat in my den, nestling my beautiful baby granddaughter in my arms. As I ran my fingers through her soft hair, the reality of my situation gripped me with great intensity. I was almost paralyzed with the thought that one day she might have to unfairly bear the agonizing consequences of her grandfather's mistake. The pain I was living with became excruciating. I fought back the tears.

My fears were well-founded. I did lose my church, my home, my possessions, and one of my greatest assets: my reputation. As the writer of Proverbs declared, "A good name is rather to be chosen than great riches" (Prov. 22:1a).

A Dangerous Foe

Fear has a way of immobilizing you and causing you to hide mistakes or failures that should be dealt with. During World War II, many of America's infantry soldiers realized that their most dangerous enemy was anxiety. If, while on the battlefield, they became gripped by the gnawing pangs of fear, they could easily forget months of training and freeze; thus giving the enemy a clear target.

Anxiety is also highly contagious. Troop commanders constantly fight against early signs of trepidation because they know how rapidly it can spread. Even though soldiers are not always aware of the reason for their fear, it can quickly snake through the ranks without any roots in reality.

Our life is much the same. You may not be engaged in a physical battle, but you are in a spiritual war. Your enemy, satan, constantly attempts to inflict you with worry and doubt of what others think about you. He also intimidates by threatening to expose your sin.

Many people have been covering their failures for so long that they are unable to recall what those mistakes were originally. This is why I use the term *inner healing* in this book. As we will see, the only effective healing is the kind that tunnels deeply into people's souls and finds the root causes of their problems. It is the key to total and complete restoration.

Worry and anxiety are not always the sources of a difficulty, but they still must be dealt with.

When fear is fueled, its haunting effects invade all your activities. It will badger you while you wash dishes, mow the lawn, or perform almost any daily task. That's why a spiritual guard must be erected in your life to protect you from its consequences. Such a fortification can only be built through the inner healing process. I call it a process because it is not always an instantaneous cure.

Deeply Rooted

When I was a young man, I developed an infection and my doctor prescribed antibiotics for me. As the days progressed I felt better, so I assumed I no longer needed to continue taking the pills. Although I honestly believed I was free of the problem, I wasn't. Only the symptoms of the illness were gone. The infection was still inflicting its destruction in my body. After a few days, the symptoms returned with even more intensity and I became seriously ill.

The doctor scolded me and said, "Marvin, I insist that you continue taking this medicine until you are completely cured." He warned me that a relapse could be life-threatening.

Many Christians fail to understand that fear should be seen as a warning signal. The real problem is deeply anchored in the soul. Only the process of healing, which most often occurs over an extended period of time, will produce permanent restoration.

Prayer, reading the Word of God, attending church, and seeking qualified counseling are all excellent. But you simply must give the Holy Spirit complete access to your life. Don't allow your difficulties to be hidden and cloaked by fear.

In the years of our ministry, Virginia and I have counseled with hundreds of individuals. This entire book could be filled with the stories of marriages that have been restored, alcoholics and drug users who have been delivered, and people who have experienced emotional and physical healing by God's divine power.

There have also been people who were within reach of victory, but somehow closed the door. Let me give you an example.

A woman I know went to a counselor who was not a Christian. She confided to this man that she had been unfaithful in her marriage. Her husband was an extremely jealous person who became angry if he even saw her talking to another man in church or at any other location. Unexpectedly, this secular counselor called the husband and informed him of her infidelity. The husband became enraged and announced that he was leaving and wanted a divorce.

I had a serious problem reconciling the two of them because the woman was distraught and fearful due to the previous insensitive disclosures to her husband by the counselor. Finally, after much encouragement, she opened up and began to talk with my wife, Virginia. However, as soon as the Holy Spirit began to gently direct her attention to the real problem, she became defensive and would not respond. She retreated into a shell of silence, saying, "I don't want to talk about it anymore." Her apprehension was constantly being fed by the action of the non-Christian counselor.

The torment she experienced overwhelmed her so much that the marriage became irreconcilable and, sadly, the couple was divorced.

I relate this story to tell you that if you allow fear to dominate your life, it can debilitate your desire to search for the root cause of your anxiety.

Listen to the words of the psalmist:

The Lord is my light and my salvation; whom shall I fear? the Lord is the strength of my life; of whom shall I be afraid? (Psalm 27:1)

Confronting Anxiety

Often the basis of our anxiety is not obvious. I knew a woman who worked in various locations as a legal secretary. She was extremely professional, always smartly dressed in a business suit. She admitted there were some issues in her life that needed to be addressed. Yet, for some reason, she was afraid to express them to me, my wife, or anyone else.

As Virginia and I prayed and discussed her situation, we tried to understand why the woman was so fearful of discussing her true concerns. Her husband was a quiet gentleman who seemed to be an example of a perfect mate.

Later we discovered that this man, who publicly appeared to be such a loving, caring person, was an extremely jealous, accusatory husband at home. She was unable to hold a job for any length of time because her husband accused her of loving every man for whom she worked. Each night her fear was ignited by his accusations, and each day she drifted further from the loving hands of Christ.

Both of these individuals had to admit and confront their anxiety before it was conquered. The Word tells us that "the Lord shall give thee rest from thy sorrow, and from thy fear..." (Is. 14:3).

If you allow such adversities to thrive, they can grow into a monster that may threaten your life. Don't wait to confront your fears, but allow the Lord to remove them in the way He chooses. Christ is still saying, "Let not your heart be troubled, neither let it be afraid" (Jn. 14:27b).

Strength in Weakness

After dealing with many troubled people and being faced with my own failure, I am convinced that we do not need to live in fear of our mistakes. God uses imperfect people.

Somehow we have come to the conclusion that God is only interested in our success, that He wants to place us in a trophy case as a flawless example of a perfected Christian life. Such a view is not consistent with the great men who are honored in the Scriptures. For our spiritual instruction, both their failures and their achievements are recorded. I am always amazed to see their weaknesses presented in such an open, honest way without embarrassment or explanation.

The apostle Peter, after numerous public outbursts, was so influenced by satan that Jesus had to rebuke him. Later, when Jesus was being tried by Pontius Pilate, Peter committed the terrible sin of denying Jesus not once, but three times.

I thought about the leniency the Lord gave to Peter when I read *Foxes' Book of Martyrs*. The book records the testimonies of thousands of Christians who were martyred because they would not deny Jesus Christ even *one* time.

Paul and Barnabas were two great missionaries who turned Asia "upside down" with the gospel of Jesus Christ. But the Word of God openly admits an argument that erupted between these two great men concerning a young minister by the name of Mark.

The Scriptures record that "the contention was so sharp between them, that they departed asunder one from the other" (Acts 15:39a). Paul chose Silas as his partner and Barnabas chose Mark. Each team continued to fulfill the Great Commission. It was years later that Paul alluded to the fact that reconciliation had occurred. In one of his letters he asked for Mark to come to him, "for he is profitable to me for the ministry"

(2 Tim. 4:11b). Their public argument had finally been resolved.

The Word also reveals that Peter, being Jewish, was prejudiced against Gentiles and would not eat with them. The apostle Paul was forced to face him on this issue and publicly rebuke him for being a hypocrite (see Gal. 2:11-14). The Bible certainly does not hide the truth about people.

Abraham, who was called "the father of the faithful" and was the patriarch of the nation of Israel, lied on two separate occasions concerning his own wife. Because of these lies, both Pharaoh, the King of Egypt, and Abimelech, the King of Geror, took her for themselves. For these mistakes, both kings were severely reprimanded by God. They in turn took reproach against Abraham.

Because of my failure, God brought me through fiery trials and difficult paths in order to cleanse and burn out the undesirable flaws of my character. As John declared, "...these things write I unto you, that ye sin not. And if any man sin, we have an advocate with the Father, Jesus Christ the righteous" (1 Jn. 2:1). This is an ongoing process necessary for all God's children.

What I am sharing with you has been branded upon my mind, my heart, and my soul by the heat of the Spirit's fire. The Scriptures declare, "Every man's work shall be made manifest: for the day shall declare it, because it shall be revealed by fire; and the fire shall try every man's work of what sort it is" (1 Cor. 3:13).

Because I experienced fear, I am now better prepared to help those who are trapped by worry and anxiety. Because I have learned how to continually experience inner healing, I can show others the path to wholeness.

Chapter 4

A Vision of Hope

"Please, Lord," I prayed, "I ask you to save the roughest sinner in New Orleans."

I was surprised by the Lord's response. Very clearly, in my spirit I heard Him say, "You're not ready for it!"

I prayed the same prayer again, but the Lord's reply did not change.

A series of events, however, let me know why the Lord had said, "You're not ready for it."

The following Sunday, during the morning service, a young lady dressed in a waitress uniform came to the altar crying. One of the parishioners whispered to me, "Pastor, she is the meanest lady in the neighborhood." I immediately thought of my prayer. It looked like we were beginning to reach some of the hardened sinners of New Orleans.

That night I was sitting on the platform beside my associate pastor when the front doors of the church opened and this same woman came down the aisle with a young woman in tow. Her guest was wearing blue "hot pants." Suddenly I became infuriated at her attire. To me it was irreverent. I grabbed the intercom phone near me and said to the startled usher, "Catch the girl in the hot pants and get her out of here!"

The usher replied anxiously, "Pastor, she's halfway down the aisle. If I remove her, it will disrupt the service. And if I catch her, what am I supposed to do with her?"

I slammed the phone down and watched in anger as the woman sat in the second row, upset that the usher did not obey me.

I was so mad that even my sermon was tinged with anger. To my amazement, the lady in the hot pants was one of the first to respond to the altar call. Soon the entire altar was filled, but no one would pray with this dear woman because they sensed my displeasure and wished to dodge my wrath. To my shame, the members of my church knew me well.

Long after the altar service ended, the woman in hot pants was still there waiting to speak to me. Evidently my message had stirred her deeply. Suddenly she noticed me trying to sneak out a side door. I was astonished when she grabbed my shoulder and screamed, "Hot dog! This is the best thing I've ever found."

Sheepishly I mumbled, "I'm glad you found Christ."

I quickly walked away, feeling offended that she did not honor our sanctuary. After all, our church was highly respected in the New Orleans Christian community. I was certain she had made some of our reputable members uncomfortable because of her inappropriate dress.

I had not, however, heard God's opinion on the subject.

The Dream

About one week later, while praying at my home, I fell into a deep sleep and had the most unusual dream.

In my mind I was transported to a brand-new medical facility, one that I was scheduled to dedicate a week later. The hospital administrator had asked me to come and tour the facility as they gave a final inspection.

As the tour began, my attention was drawn to several things. The administrator was a middle-aged man who weighed about 180 pounds. He stood nearly six feet tall and was dressed in a navy blue pin-striped suit. The gray around his temples gave him a "Donald Trump" appearance.

In my dream, the tour began on the top floor. I was impressed by the orderliness of the facility: custom carpets, elegant drapes, expensive scenic pictures, and spotless hallways. The nurses' stations were equipped with the latest computer terminals. Everything was engineered to enhance the efficiency of patient care and administration. The rooms were of such high fashion that even the pillows on the bed were tucked in a manner reminiscent of the attention to minute details in a five-star hotel.

The tour seemed endless. Finally, the smartly dressed administrator spun on his heels and exclaimed, "Let me show you my pride and joy."

We passed through a group of swinging doors down a long corridor. I heard the sound of our heels clicking against the mirror-finished floor. For a moment I stopped and saw the reflection of my smile on the floor.

As the dream continued we approached two large, gleaming, stainless steel doors which opened inward, revealing the cleanest room I had ever seen. The counters were polished to a chrome-like sheen and the instrument racks shined.

The administrator proudly showed me the latest equipment and explained the various functions of the high-tech machines. While we were engrossed in conversation, I heard the distant screams of sirens and interrupted our discussion. I asked, "Don't you think those sirens are coming toward us?"

"Reverend, I think you're right," he responded.

We both rushed toward the Emergency Room. Through the glass exit doors we looked to see five ambulances pulling into the carport in front of us. The administrator and I exchanged glances of deep concern. There must have been some horrible accident just a short distance away.

Attendants began rushing toward the emergency door with stretchers. On one was a girl with sandy-red hair whose right arm was broken. An exposed bone was protruding out of the wound and blood was pouring from cuts along her ear, mouth, and scalp. On a stretcher beside her was a woman in her mid-thirties. Her dark hair was tangled and matted with blood. She must have been the mother of the other patient because her hand was reaching out to the girl. The mother's leg was also broken, and lay awkwardly across her other leg.

I stood there with a stunned look, viewing the mass suffering in front of me, as the area became filled with stretchers and the cries of the wounded. A driver grabbed the administrator and screamed, "Hurry! Open the emergency room doors before these people die."

He replied, "You can't bring these dirty, bloody people in here and mess up my clean and sterile hospital."

The driver desperately pleaded, "We have just a few minutes or these people will die, and their blood will be on your hands."

I could hold my silence no longer. I caught the administrator by the shoulders and spoke directly into his face. "You cannot turn these people away. This hospital was built to save lives."

I began to shake him, screaming, "Take these people into the hospital!"

God's Infirmary

Suddenly, I awoke and found myself back in my living room, drenched in sweat. As I tried to regain my composure, the Lord spoke to me: "The church was built as a hospital for the sin-sick. No one should have to clean up or get better before they come. You are to accept them as they are. Allow them to enter and bring them to healing."

As I lay there on the couch, the dream began to revolutionize my thinking. I had asked the Lord to save the roughest person in New Orleans, yet I was not even prepared to welcome a lady in hot pants to our church. No wonder God said I wasn't ready for such a person to be saved.

If the Church is not careful, it will forget its true purpose in society. God's house is not a museum; it is a hospital. Broken, flawed, and temperamental people need to be assured that the church is a sanctuary, a haven of refuge that will always welcome them, regardless of their circumstances.

I was now beginning to understand what Jesus meant the Church to be. God used a vivid dream to show me the profound truth that His house is to be a hospital to heal the wounded.

Jesus spoke directly to the subject when the Pharisees asked Him why He spent time with people who had serious problems. He declared, "...They that be whole need not a physician, but they that are sick. But go ye and learn what that meaneth, I will have mercy, and not sacrifice: for I am not come to call the righteous, but sinners to repentance" (Mt. 9:12-13).

He Wept Silently

In the darkest hours of my crisis many scenes of my life came before me. One face in particular haunted me. It was of a man in Africa for whom the Church had become a spiritual shelter.

In Nairobi, Kenya, there is a simple but sturdy brick structure that houses the East African School of Theology. This training center has sent native missionaries throughout the entire continent of Africa. Kenya has always been considered a "free" country because inhabitants of other African countries can travel there with minimal restrictions. My church had contributed heavily to this bastion of Christian education. I remembered walking down the hallways of the school, smelling that earthy, hot, muggy air blowing through the shuttered windows, thinking, "I must do all I can to advance this vital part of God's Kingdom."

I was asked to speak at the school's dedication service. One of the soloists in the choir was a young African student with chalky white teeth. With deep conviction he sang the familiar song, "His Eye Is on the Sparrow."

During my message, this student wept silently as he sat on the front row. The moment the service concluded he ran over to me, gave me a bear hug, and exclaimed, "Pastor Gorman, I escaped from Ethiopia, leaving my wife and two-year-old son behind. I walked many days to come to this school and I know the call of God is on my life. I want to thank you for helping to build this great institute."

I placed my hand against his bronze cheek and became so choked with emotion that I could not speak. With a knowing glance he broke the awkward silence. "It is all right, Pastor, for soon I will be back with my family and I will preach the gospel just like you."

He returned to his famine-ridden nation to build a church, one of the Lord's spiritual hospitals, where the sick and wounded find salvation and healing.

When my world came crashing down, I again saw this young man's face before me. I earnestly prayed, "Lord, don't allow him to see my failure. Let him see Jesus, the Great Physician, the Deliverer, the Healer of broken hearts."

Chapter 5

A Prophetic Warning

There were divine inklings that an impending disaster was about to explode in my life. The problem was, I was so caught up in the success of our church that I did not heed the warnings. The prophet Amos declared, "Surely the Lord God will do nothing, but He revealeth His secret unto His servants the prophets" (Amos 3:7).

The first premonition that something was amiss came on August 29, 1982, during a service at our church with Mario Murillo, a well-known West Coast evangelist. Mario stepped to the platform and began his sermon with boldness and cutting clarity. His message was entitled, "Cross Over," and I want to share these excerpts.

I'm going to tell you a story. And I want to tell it as a parable.

First Assembly of God is a great church. Imagine, if you will, one day this man [Marvin Gorman] was arrested, taken miles from here, and put in jail. The church body was suddenly under the care of all the pastors that this man had raised up. The body suddenly was in a position where it no longer had the luxury of this man's authority in the pulpit, and everyone suddenly had to remember what they were taught. Everything that was symbolic, now comes home. Suddenly Brother Gorman's love for this church is verified.

Sometimes you don't know what you've got till you lose it.

He's in jail now and seven men, not from this body, but from the outside, who have had jealousy, hatred, and malice in their hearts toward this man, come into this church. They are eloquent, they are powerful, they are convincing, and they cut the church up into seven pieces, so that now there's only a handful meeting in this building, and the rest are scattered all over New Orleans.

Word gets back to him a year later that the great work for God that he built is cut up seven ways, like a pie. The first reaction would be the horror, anger, and resentment that Brother Gorman would feel for those seven men. Then, secondly, the resentment of how quickly those who had sat for years under his ministry could be deluded by someone else.

One of the men was saying that Brother Gorman was in jail because of secret sin in his heart, and that in his absence God had "raised us up to take over."

I want you to know what helplessness is. Helplessness is a feeling you get when you watch somebody you love get hurt, yet you can't do anything about it. Paul saw the church he loved divided while he was in a prison cell.

Now, the first thing you go through is rage. Brother, I pray that God never tests this man [pointing to Brother Gorman] *this way. Because you know what? After everything is said and done, there's one thing that makes you come here Sunday after Sunday. You know he loves you. You know he does. And that doesn't come with the territory, because I am in a lot of churches where the men don't.*

The physical agony of being in jail was something that Paul didn't consider, because his heart was in his throat over the reports that the church was now meeting in seven places under the teaching of heretics.

Paul's first outrage was toward those seven men.

His second outrage was to the church, for not knowing that God raised him up and that he was an apostle of God. Do you know he [Paul] got reports back that the Philippians no longer believed he was a man of God?

But the third thing was what Paul could have felt toward the Lord. Because he said, "Why, God, would You have arrested me now? How could You have let these pagans come and get me at the one time the church needed me the most?"

God was going to show something to Paul and he could have blown it.

The mother eagle teaches the baby eagle to fly in the most incredible way. There's a lot of "down" and feathers in the eagle's nest way up in the mountains, thousands of feet up. And when it's time for the babies to learn how to fly, the mother jumps up on top of the nest and starts beating all the down out of it; just blows it out with those huge wings until the briery thorns are exposed and the eaglets are encouraged to leave. They climb on the mother and she soars straight up and then drops them. This is a very rude introduction to flight.

The question is: Do you think of the mother eagle as being cruel? Yes, if you have limited information. Because it takes love to test somebody you love. It takes love to take them out of your bosom and say, "You've got to stand on your feet, and since I love you, I am going to prepare you for life."

The third aspect is like a cruise missile. We have the most advanced jet airplanes in the world. We have a space shuttle that is absolutely years ahead of anything the Russians have. But nothing we've ever built that flies has the accuracy of a mother eagle coming down out of the [heights] to pick up her eaglets before they hit the ground.

They say you will never live to see a more incredible sight than that. She'll catch them. But the ones that aren't trying to learn to fly, and don't flap their wings, are the ones that are going to fall the longest before they're caught. That's why we prolong our suffering.

God shook up your life, shook you out of the nest to get you into His Word, to get wrong attitudes out of you. And you're going to keep plummeting to the earth until you say, "Lord, I'm going to flap my wings. I'm going to use my character."

Now, the most dangerous thing of all is when the person rejects the process of God's correction altogether, and literally fights the mother eagle off and hits the ground.

The question is this: Would God sacrifice a whole church in order to do something in Paul's character? The answer is "Yes!"

Paul's only comfort was his discovery. And the magnificent spirit that came out of that cell has never been equaled. There's never been a Christian like Paul.

Let's look at his three outrages.

> Number 1. How could these seven men do this to me?
>
> Number 2. How could the church forget so readily?
>
> Number 3. How could God let this happen to me?

How many of you have ever asked those questions? How many of you have ever asked why your friends could do something to you? How could people lie about you? How many of you have ever been gossiped about behind your back? How many of you get a sick feeling in your stomach when that happens?

In Philippians chapter 1, God took Paul through the process of healing. I want to make this point clear. **Always give God the benefit of the doubt. Never insult God's character. Never!**

And Paul trusted God, forgave the Philippians, and got rid of all the animosity against those other preachers.

If you have ever loved somebody and they've broken your heart, their memory when it comes to you is a pain. You don't want to remember.

*The healing of Paul's bitterness was so complete that he was able to say, "I thank God every time I remember you." Every time he would remember, it would bring back the tragedy, but his spirit was so healed in God that he said, "I am able to praise God that I remember you because **I have crossed over!**"*

*When Paul crossed over, he got something else: "Being confident of this...that He which hath begun a good work in you will complete it" [see Phil. 1:6]. Paul had learned the secret of the mother eagle. God will shake the Church, let her fall, let her crumble, but **He will never let His Church hit the ground.**

God began First Assembly. God started this church at Philippi. Paul said, "I don't care if you get one thousand heretics, because I know who started this church, and Jesus who began it will protect it and make it grow. I know that now." And he said, "Maybe all I can do at this time is write letters."

By God delivering us from our subjective, senti-mental attachment to the now, He can lift us up and build in us a character whose impact will be eternal. If Paul had rejected God's counsel or did not ask for greatness, he would have stayed out of jail and built a fine church at Philippi. But we never would have had the Philippian letter and it would not have influenced the billions of lives that would come later. The biggest flaw with a positive confession is that it removes the power of God to do those kinds of things in you. Because if you ask God, you will actually ask Him to avoid suffering. You know you will.

I know I will. I know if I say, "God, I want to control my life and destiny by my own prayers and my own way," I'll never see the surprises that are down the road.

Folks, that's a heavy truth. It hurts. Is this the kind of relationship you want? Well, you can start victimizing the devil. **Cross over!**

Not Chance Events

To be honest, as I listened to the message of Mario Murillo, I knew God was trying to tell me something but I did not know the full ramifications of what it was. At that time our church seemed to be in an unshakable position. As I sat there on the platform, I thought, "How awful it would be if something this devastating happened to me or to anyone else."

Mario's illustration of suffering was powerful, but I'm sure no one in our congregation, especially me, believed that his sermon was prophetic in nature.

That night the Holy Spirit was stirring inside me and I vividly recall falling on my knees at the end of the sermon and making a new commitment to the Lord.

Several months after I was forced to leave First Assembly of God, this message became an important piece of the puzzle I was attempting to reconstruct. A close friend said, "Marvin, do you remember the sermon that Mario preached, comparing you with the apostle Paul in jail?"

My wife and I quickly scrambled through our tape library and when we found our copy of the sermon, we played it over and over. It became a beacon of encouragement assuring us that many of the difficult things we experienced were not chance events; they were crafted by the hand of a loving God.

In the Lord's own unique ways, He forewarns us of events that are on the horizon. His warnings may be words of caution or words of edification. He may speak directly to our heart or speak through the words of one of His servants. Our responsibility is to listen.

To Be Free

Less than three weeks before the storm hit my life with gale force, God gave me another warning. While I was flying to a camp meeting in Oregon, I closed my eyes and began to pray. I had just finished reading a book by Andrew Murray, *Intercessory Prayer*, and was overwhelmed with a hunger to be in the presence of God. I began to cry with such heartfelt emotion that I was fearful a flight attendant might notice me and think I was ill. I turned and rested my head on the window as my body shook with sobs.

"Lord," I prayed, "I am so tired of endless board meetings, committee reports, and politics that are draining the life out of me. Please, I want to be free to just pray and preach Your Word."

I paused for a moment. In the silence that followed the Lord spoke: "Would you be willing to leave the Assemblies of God?"

"Lord, what does that have to do with anything?" I responded.

Finally I said, "Lord, I will do anything! I'll go anywhere, but I just want to be free."

At that time I did not know the importance of my conversation with the Lord. Now, in retrospect, I realize God was making a covenant with me and cautioning me that within just a few weeks almost everything that I loved would be taken away.

The last warning that the Lord gave me happened the night before I received the telephone call that ended my ministry at the First Assembly of God. I was preaching a message entitled, "For His Great Name's

Sake." In the sermon I kept emphasizing the point that God will not forsake you, "for His Name's sake." I quoted the prophet Moses as he spoke to the people of Israel: "The Lord did not set His love upon you, nor choose you, because ye were more in number than any people; for ye were the fewest of all people" (Deut. 7:7).

"We are all in pressure boxes," I told the congregation, "and some may not know how to cope. I have learned how to pray and turn my predicaments over to Jesus."

For some reason, in the middle of the message, I closed my Bible and gave an altar call. A number of people were saved. When I walked to my office, I did not realize that it would be the last time I would preach as the pastor of that church. As I was putting my sermon notes away, suddenly the Lord impressed upon me: "Mark your notes and date them. You will finish this sermon at a later time."

Chapter 6

The Road to Repentance

"Ask whatever you want," I told the counselor. "I promise I won't hold anything back." Virginia and I were in Akron, Ohio, meeting with the well-known Christian psychologist, Dr. Richard Dobbins.

When my ministry came to an abrupt halt in July, 1986, the board of the church arranged for my wife and me to spend some time in counseling. It was a necessary step on my path to healing.

Arriving at his complex in Akron, we were warmly greeted by Dr. Dobbins and his caring staff. He is a very sensitive, Spirit-filled Christian.

Without fanfare the questioning began. My desire for repentance was so great that I was determined to be totally open and candid and share every fact I could remember.

After several days of extremely painful questioning and counseling, I felt as transparent as a clear windowpane. I thought Dr. Dobbins had explored every possible avenue of forgiveness and repentance, but I discovered this was just the beginning. He said, "I believe it would be helpful for your three children to fly here and become part of these sessions."

Randy, Mark, and Beverly, along with their spouses soon joined us. I can vividly recall the day I was seated in a chair, encircled by my wife and family. For the next two hours the children were encouraged to ask me any question that came to their mind, no matter how embarrassing. It was a somber moment of truth.

The encounter was to ensure that everything was openly aired and discussed and that there were no shady-gray areas of doubt remaining among any of the family members. The questions often stung me with the anguish any father would feel when the innermost areas of his behavior are being exposed to the children he cares for so deeply. I fought against the tormenting thought, "How could my children ever love me again?"

The second day's meeting with my family and Dr. Dobbins dealt with our healing process and how each individual had been affected by what had occurred. The week the story broke, one of my sons had been so strongly interrogated about my life by men who had once been our friends, that he began to sob and fell to the floor. My other son was so devastated by the shock of it all that he required medication.

The sessions in Akron, although agonizing, gave my family the assurance that I wasn't hiding anything else from them.

Returning home, we again had another lengthy family discussion. I wanted to make it absolutely clear that they could approach me at any time to inquire about things that might be bothering them. We made a covenant with each other that any gossip or rumors we heard would only be discussed among ourselves.

Mending Broken Vessels

It is impossible for those who don't know Christ to comprehend why a person would be willing to confess his faults if there is a chance of having his reputation ruined. Satan constantly encourages us to protect our image and make ourselves "look good." How do we destroy his control over us? It is by telling the truth and allowing light to shine into the deepest crevices of our lives. To be effective, repentance must be complete, open, and honest.

There is a town in Switzerland that is renowned for its delicate and beautiful urns. When you travel to this quaint village, you learn the lengthy, detailed process the urns go through on their path to completion. The potter takes a huge lump from the purest clay and places it on the wet potter's wheel. For hours the stoop-shouldered artist shapes the sides of the vase until it stands nearly as tall as his own height. He allows the vessel to sit for a week before he applies multiple coats of glaze to the outside surface. Then he fires the vase in a huge brick kiln heated to nearly 2,000 degrees.

After the urn has cooled, the potter places it into a special, clean room. He then takes an old sledge hammer and breaks the crafted container into hundreds of pieces! For the next two weeks the potter painstakingly glues the urn back together with gold filigree. Something that was beautiful becomes exquisite after it is broken and repaired by the gifted craftsman.

So it is with life. Character is molded by our heavenly Potter's hands.

A female evangelist once described a vision in which she saw her life as a vase resting upon a counter in the temple of the Lord. Suddenly, to her dismay, the vessel slipped off the ledge and smashed to pieces on the floor. She began to cry when she saw her life so shattered. The Lord gently reached down and patiently picked up the pieces, saying, "Here, daughter, this is your life. I have put it back together."

The woman had been sobbing because she felt so useless after being broken. In her vision, the Lord tapped her shoulder and continued, "You don't understand. When I place My light inside your vase, the broken lines will disappear as My glory shines through the cracks."

It is through the broken places in our lives, in the areas mended through repentance, that others can see the glory of God.

You may have sinned through transgressions that include stealing, lying, or cheating, but when you truly repent, you allow the glorious light of God to radiate through your imperfections.

A Change of Mind

The Greeks have a word to describe a force so powerful that it dramatically produces a change of action. The word is *metanoeo* and it means "a change of mind." It is derived from two words: *meta*, which means above or beyond (for example, from the normal to the supernatural), and *noia*, from the root *nous*, which refers to the exercise of the mind.

One use of the word has its origins in the Greek Olympics. If a young runner was unable to improve his previous record, his coach would decide that he needed to experience a *metanoeo*. One day the coach would loose a tiger in the vicinity of the unsuspecting athlete. When the young man heard the growls of the pursuing animal, he would suddenly have a change of mind that quickly resulted in a change of action.

In Peter Senge's best-seller, *The Fifth Discipline*, he discusses the need for a radical reconsideration of reasoning in business that will revolutionize the entire corporate structure. To launch his five-day seminars, he uses the same Greek word: *metanoeo*. He calls it one of the most powerful and positive words in any language.

No wonder John the Baptist chose *metanoeo* to be the first word uttered when he preached. Christ Himself chose this as the initial word He spoke when He began His ministry to mankind: "Repent: for the kingdom of heaven is at hand" (Mt. 4:17b).

The true meaning of the word for "repentance" was a revelation to me when I first learned it. For years the Church has tried to limit the definition of repentance to the words, "I am sorry," with a promise not to repeat the offense. In reality, repentance is a more comprehensive term. It is complete submission of one's mental processes to God, which results in a transformation by His pervasive power. Repentance leads to an in-depth change of both attitude and activity.

There is no substitute for a serious prayer session that includes tears of confession while pouring your heart out to God. In the early days of Pentecostal churches this was called "praying through." It is a process that breaks emotional barriers in the heart that withhold honesty and truth from the Lord. I've heard older ministers try to explain the experience by saying, "It is better felt than 'telt.' "

You can't learn to swim by watching a teacher diagram a backstroke on a chalkboard. No explanation, no matter how eloquent, could ever describe the actual experience of being totally submerged while trying to propel your body through the water. The only way to learn to "dog-paddle" or tread water is to jump into the pool and do it.

True repentance begins when you enter into your prayer closet or respond to a church altar call and empty your soul to God. Then you will know what it means to have the Lord cleanse your soul.

A Prolonged Process

"Pastor, will I ever stop crying?" asked a woman named Mickey.

I had been counseling her for several weeks and knew she had hurtful memories from the past that continued to torment and haunt her. Although the emotional trauma had taken place long ago, it remained fresh in her mind.

Mickey is a dedicated woman who is loyal to our church. Her husband is a captain with a local fire department. While counseling her, the Holy Spirit began to reveal to me that repentance is not always an instant event, but rather a continuing process. It is through long-term repentance that the Holy Spirit can reveal the deeper problems that are the true causes of our present situation.

In Mickey's case, God spoke to me to ask her to repent for 15 minutes, three times a day. As she prayed,

God began to gently disclose other faults that needed to be addressed and remedied. As the process continued, it became easier and easier for her to confront her past problems.

Many people make the mistake of looking at repentance as a one-time event, but in reality it is an on-going process.

The Wrong Direction

In the Old Testament there is a story of a prophet named Jonah, who lived about 760 B.C. Jonah, a godly man, wished to do his best to please the Lord. One day God commanded Jonah: "Arise, go to Nineveh, that great city, and cry against it; for their wickedness is come up before Me" (Jon. 1:2). He rebelled against the Lord's directive.

Nineveh was a city in the Syrian empire. These long-standing enemies of Israel were pagans and worshiped false gods. They also had a history of taking Israelites captive and forcing them to submit to the humiliation of idol worship. Jonah wondered, "Why should I be saddled with the task of going to the most deplorable people on earth and warning them of God's impending destruction?" He felt they would only mock his sincerity.

Jonah took leave of his better judgment and fled from the presence of the Lord. Running from his native village of Gath-Hepher, he crossed the low rolling

Judean hills to the Mediterranean Sea. Coming upon the city of Haifa, he found a rustic maritime ship that was headed in the opposite direction from Nineveh, toward the northern city of Tarsus.

As Jonah steadied himself against the rolling seas he thought, "I am a patriot and the love of Israel beats within my heart. The nation of Israel has suffered innumerable atrocities from the Assyrians. The sooner God destroys this godless nation, the better. Why should I warn them? God might then show them mercy and prolong their existence as an enemy of my people."

Jonah's lack of enthusiasm to perform God's task was based upon, as some would say, good moral judgment. What he forgot was that the Lord loves all people and is not willing that any should perish, even if they are your enemies.

Soon the ship carrying Jonah was tossed about in a turbulent, destructive sea. The men of the ship, fearing for their lives, concluded that the storm was the result of God's displeasure. They chose to cast lots among all who were on board to see if the offending party could be found.

The lot fell upon Jonah and he confessed that he was the man. He asked them to cast his body into the raging sea—then all would be well. To the shock and amazement of the seafaring merchants, when helpless Jonah was tossed alive into the sea, a huge fish rose out of the billowing waves and swallowed him whole. Jonah was carried in the belly of this fish on a three-day journey. Finally the fish spit him onto the sandy shores of the Israelite coast. Jonah then faced a 350-mile journey to the city of Nineveh. The digestive juices inside the huge fish had bleached his skin to a chalky white; his appearance was both frightening and alarming, but his message was clear. All who saw him knew this man was on a mission from God.

Sackcloth and Soul-Searching

In the Bible Nineveh was called "a great city." This could also be translated as "a city important to God." I can see the king of Nineveh adjusting his robes as he walked out onto his balcony that overlooked the massive expanse of his beloved city. From wall to wall the city was nearly 60 miles across and the walls were so massive that the king could ride his chariot along the top of them with his two generals in chariots of their own at his sides.

Perhaps he wondered, "Why is there so much sin in our camp? What has caused my people to sink so low?"

His thoughts were interrupted by a messenger who no doubt fell to his knees and exclaimed, "Oh King, live forever! There is a man of ghastly appearance—a Jewish prophet—and he has declared these words, 'Yet forty days, and Nineveh shall be overthrown.' "

The king was shocked. Had this prophet been reading his own thoughts? He had heard how the God of the Jews was like no other god, and that their prophets were known to be so accurate that if one varied from the truth, he would be stoned immediately and left for dead. The king knew the words of Jonah were from God.

Suddenly the palace was filled with a whirlwind of activity. Locks were placed on all the cupboards and the sellers of food were cleared from the street. Every man, woman, and child was commanded to remove their apparel and dress in the clothing of death—in sackcloth.

The great city of Nineveh declared a fast that included even the cattle. No living thing was to eat a morsel of food until the 40 days had passed. Each day the king came before his court and had his scribes declare again his decree:

> "...Let neither man nor beast, herd nor flock, taste any thing: let them not feed, nor drink water: but let man and beast be covered with sackcloth, and cry mightily unto God: yea, let them turn every one from his evil way, and from the violence that is in their hands. Who can tell if God will turn and repent, and turn away from His fierce anger, that we perish not?" (Jonah 3:7-9).

The people of Nineveh continued to repent day after day. God heard their cry and spared the city. If this pagan king understood the drastic measures that repentance required, how much more should we understand the significance of repentance in our lives?

This story should serve as a reminder that repentance is not merely mumbling a few conscience-stricken apologies. It is a process of daily soul-searching to uncover areas of our lives that have not yet been committed to God. As each layer of remorse is peeled away, we will be closer to the source of our sinfulness and the origin of our stress and sorrow.

Following my storm, I began to read the Book of Jonah and was struck by the parallels that Jonah and I had both experienced. God allowed me to sail in the opposite direction also. I filed a lawsuit against Jimmy Swaggart, his ministry, and others. He also made plain the verse, "All things are lawful unto me, but all things are not expedient" (1 Cor. 6:12a).

It was in the belly of the fish where Jonah surrendered all to the will and purpose of God. However, he was helpless to free himself until God allowed it. The embarrassment, humiliation, and stress of the lawsuit were overwhelming. Like Jonah, I was helpless to free myself until the process ran its course. It was during this period of time that I was able to deal with many of my inner struggles, in order for my life to be completely yielded to Him. I do not believe that everyone has to have a "Jonah experience." However, there is a process of breaking and molding that we must all go through in order to become more useful in His Kingdom.

I have seen people come to church expecting to receive instantaneous deliverance and healing from problems that have plagued them for years. Yes, God forgives our sin instantly and demons can be cast out without delay. The *effects* of sin, however, are deeply rooted in one's personality. Sins are transgressional in nature and are removed by the *process* of repentance.

Have you had a *metanoeo* experience? My friend, you can know a repentance so powerful that the entire course of your life will have a new direction.

Chapter 7

Searching for the Source

It was during the evening service at First Assembly in New Orleans that the sound of a gunshot echoed throughout the auditorium. Immediately a hushed silence fell over the entire congregation and all eyes turned toward the balcony. Several of us hurriedly climbed the stairs to the location of the outburst. There on the floor was a 14-year-old boy, dead from a self-inflicted wound!

The young man was not a member of our congregation. He was brought to the service by one of our families. As he was sitting in church, depression overcame him to the point that he took his own life.

Upon investigation, the sad facts became known. I was told that the boy's mother had remarried, and just a few days before this tragedy, the father had also married again. Following his dad's wedding, the young man was placed in a foster home. These events caused him to sink into a state of deep depression.

His feelings of rejection and self-pity were the perfect environment for satan to fill the boy with deep anger. His hostility escalated out of control and he made the tragic decision to take his own life.

Living With Anger

I know what it means to struggle with intense anger.

The Arkansas farmhouse in which I was raised holds many memories, and not all of them are pleasant. My father was an alcoholic. His dependence on alcohol robbed him of his ability to adequately take care of his family; thus, we were always lacking financially.

Daddy was a small man, weighing less than 140 pounds, but he was extremely strong-willed. He worked as a logging estimator. He was able to mentally calculate how many board feet of wood could be obtained out of an acre of forest. His potential, however, was always thwarted by his desperate craving for alcohol.

I was constantly tormented by the feeling that people were rejecting me because of my father. It continually caused my anger to flare.

After I was married and left home, my anger continued. Often I asked the Lord to identify the fuel that ignited my resentment. Then, as I sought God's face following my fall, He brought me back to a night when I was just eight years old.

There was no electricity on our farm and our rough-board house was lit by kerosene lamps and by flickering flames from the brick fireplace. Very early one morning I was getting dressed in the corner of my room, watching the shadows dance upon the walls. I heard my father in the next room cursing my mother. With fear flooding my young mind, I wanted to do something—anything—to stop the onslaught of my father's obscenities against my mother. I firmly believe that what happened in those days became the root of my future problems.

Even at that tender age, anger against my father began to build within me and intensified over the passing years. The rage that began in that farmhouse grew to become a huge, poisonous tree in my spirit.

For many years, the resentment had been suppressed. Then, in 1987, as part of my healing process, I searched my spirit and discovered that this root of anger was still very much alive and had to be dealt with. I had to cut the tree down and expose its roots. The Lord showed me there wasn't only one incident that needed to be dealt with, but it was one of many.

More Than a Dream

When I was 20 years old I was working as a single pastor, living with a family about 20 miles from my parents. One night in prayer the Lord revealed something to me that was quite unusual. Very clearly, I saw my father, stranded in his truck, and I knew he needed my help.

I got into my car and drove to the spot the Lord had shown me. I arrived at an abandoned gravel pit and there was my father sleeping in his red International pickup truck. The engine was still running. The rear wheels had slipped off the gravel road into a ditch. As I tried to awaken my dad, I saw that his feet and ankles had turned blue from the icy rain and cold. The temperature was hovering around 27 degrees.

When I looked down at my father, I could feel the fury within rising once again—not directed at him specifically, but at what alcohol was doing to him. I took him to the warmth and comfort of his home.

Finally the day came when I asked the Lord to remove the anger from me that began so long ago. I felt a tremendous rush of freedom and experienced the full meaning of the words of Jesus: "If the Son therefore shall make you free, ye shall be free indeed" (Jn. 8:36).

Why did these roots have to be removed? They were fueling my resentment and anger, and were hindering my recovery.

Fifteen years after the pickup truck incident, I drove approximately 350 miles to my father's hospital room and listened to the physician explain that my dad had a cancerous mass in his lungs. The doctor took me aside and said, "Son, your dad only has about three months to live." Then he placed his hand on my shoulder and quietly told me, "I have never seen a father who admires his son as much as your father admires you."

No one will ever know how that statement moved me. My dad had a very difficult time paying me a compliment.

I purchased a Bible as a gift for him and brought it to the hospital. When I placed it on his tray, the pages fell open to the words of Jesus in the Book of John, which I began to read aloud, "Him that cometh to Me I will in no wise cast out" (Jn. 6:37b).

My father hesitantly asked, "Bud, does that mean me?"

"Yes, Dad, it does," I gladly told him.

During the next few minutes I was able to lead my father to Jesus Christ. He lived several more months. It was so rewarding to enjoy him as the Christian father I had always longed for. Christ gave us a love for each other that I wish every father and son could experience.

Forgiving Ourselves

Anger is not only produced by the actions of others, but by our own deeds. When we sin, for example, there is a constant self-hatred within us for allowing failure. After we ask the Lord's forgiveness for the transgressions we have committed, we must then forgive ourselves.

If internal strife is allowed to continue, the result will be intolerance toward others, a tendency to judge them severely because of their failures and shortcomings. I now realize that until my problems came to the surface, my anger was often directed toward people I counseled, including staff members and those in my own family. More than once, I have deeply regretted my actions and have asked forgiveness.

Anger brings out the ugliest characteristics of our life. It certainly had that effect on me.

Usually I could control myself while in the pulpit, but I was constantly aware that this fury pressured me to live on the edge of explosion. It was a continual fight to control and suppress it. Unfortunately, I sometimes lost the battle.

The anger I am talking about promotes self-justification, self-righteousness, and, worst of all, pride.

All these things the Lord slowly brought to light during the beginning years of my repentance and inner healing. The lonely hours of prayer and intimacy allowed the Father of Light to shine His glory into the corners of my heart and expose areas where satan had gained his evil footholds.

The apostle Paul addressed this subject when he wrote to the people at the church in Ephesus, "Be ye angry, and sin not: let not the sun go down upon your wrath: neither give place to the devil" (Eph. 4:26-27).

I have met people who use this verse to justify anger. Some things in life will enrage you, but don't let the sun go down on your wrath. If you do, you will be giving an invitation to satan.

The original Greek word for "place" is *topos*. It is where we get our English "topography," which is the science of representing surface features of a region on maps, charts, or a piece of real estate. Paul is saying that if you allow the sun to set on anger, you have given satan a property deed to your spirit. When that happens, the devil will have access to your heart and will attempt to control all areas of your life.

It's time to be totally honest with your past. Address the issues that harm your emotions and ask God to bury them in His sea of forgetfulness. You'll be able to say:

"Let all bitterness, and wrath, and anger, and clamour, and evil speaking, be put away from you, with all malice: and be ye kind one to another, tenderhearted, forgiving one another, even as God for Christ's sake hath forgiven you" (Ephesians 4:31-32).

Finding the source of your anger is only a prelude to discovering the source of your deliverance.

Chapter 8

Eye to Eye With Satan

Several years ago a woman contacted me over a period of several weeks, trying to make an appointment for counseling. Since she was a member of another church in our city, I felt hesitant in scheduling an appointment.

Finally, I told her if she brought a letter from her pastor giving me permission to counsel her, I would do so. Her pastor relayed the message that the reason he wanted me to counsel this woman was because she was dealing with demons. He felt I was the only person in New Orleans who knew how to handle this matter.

"I have a serious problem, Pastor Gorman," the woman said as she came into my office for her appointment. She was extremely depressed. "I have 29 demons. My prayer group has discovered all of them," she stated.

The woman opened her purse and pulled out a piece of church stationary on which was written the list of "demons." As I scanned the list, I noted that one of the demons specified was gluttony. The woman only weighed about 130 pounds and was approximately 5'5". I thought, "Either someone missed that one or the demon of gluttony that is possessing her isn't doing his job." Also listed were the demons of lust, jealousy, hate, and many more.

"I won't agree to pray against any of these," I said, handing the note back to her.

"But, Brother Gorman, my pastor and my prayer group discerned these," she desperately exclaimed.

"I don't mean to criticize," I replied, "but God does not give anyone the ability to identify a demon if He doesn't also give that person the power to cast it out of an individual who wants to be free. These so-called demons are not the cause of your conflicts."

As I spoke these words, the Lord suddenly whispered in my spirit that her problems stemmed from something that had happened in her teens. Following several sessions of counseling, I eventually discovered that she had long-standing bitterness and anger toward her stepmother for acts of cruelty the woman had inflicted on her during her teenage years. When this resentment was brought to light, she began to weep.

I was able to lead the woman in a prayer of repentance that was the beginning of the process that brought her to total victory. The symptoms she thought were demonic also left when she truly repented.

Much damage has been done to the Body of Christ by those who claim that Christians are or can be possessed by demons. In an attempt to explain how sin can enter a child of God after conversion, some Bible teachers believe you can be filled with the Holy Ghost and be possessed by demons at the same time.

That is a dangerous theology and I have seen that teaching cause many unnecessary problems in the Church. In some cases, innocent Christians open up their spirit to fleshly actions that appear to be demonic. As we all know, the power of suggestion can be very persuasive.

Advice From Aunt Polly

On our Arkansas farm, my family raised pigs. I remember the nanny we had, whose name was Aunt Polly Moore, a thin woman in her 80's with short, gray hair. She was 16 years old when she was freed from slavery.

Aunt Polly loved our hogs. "Watch this," she told me. I observed with great curiosity as she put lye in their food. "The pigs are going to squeal, but it will be good for them because this stuff kills the parasites," she explained.

In the next pen there was some hog meal that didn't have lye in it. Our large female pig, called "Mama Hog," knew that's where the better-tasting food was. Whenever Aunt Polly tried to feed her the lye-laced food, Mama Hog would break down the fence and head straight for the untreated food. It seemed that no matter how strong the fence was, it could not hold her.

One day, as I was trying to repair the fence, Aunt Polly saw my frustration and yelled to me. "Baby," she said, "a stronger fence isn't what you need. You've just got to remove that hog feed!"

More than once, when I encounter people who mistakenly believe they are possessed with demons, I think about those hogs. If a person removes the unrepentant sin that is feeding his thoughts, the demonic forces will not be breaking down the fences to torment and oppress him.

Seeking Vengeance

One of the most dangerous attitudes your spirit can harbor is that of bitterness. Allowing bitterness to dominate your life is like throwing out a welcome mat and inviting every demon who walks by to come inside.

Far too often I meet bitter people who say, "I'm justified. I have a right to be this way! That person wronged me and if I am going to stand up for what is right, I must seek vengeance." These attitudes permeate our society.

In countless action movies, the plot revolves around a great injustice that has been done to the hero. As the drama unfolds, the problems mount and it looks like he won't get his chance to retaliate. Then comes the final scene. The hero, while blasting holes in buildings, kills all the villains and takes vengeance into his own hands. By the time the credits are ready to roll, the main character has married the leading lady, is basking in wealth, and winks at the way he has handled justice.

If you believe that scenario represents real life, I have a bridge that I would like to sell you in the Sahara Desert.

It is usually the opposite that occurs. After an injustice, we look for vengeance. When our attempts backfire, we are embarrassed and become more angry and even more bitter. This opens the door for demonic activity that can lead to demon possession if genuine repentance is not experienced.

Seeds of Rebellion

Let me share a little-known story from the Bible that illustrates the danger of such bitterness.

King David, one of Israel's greatest leaders, employed a wise counselor by the name of Ahithophel. He was a familiar figure in David's court and often advised him concerning the affairs of his kingdom. Ahithophel's proposals were so profound that it was "as if a man had inquired at the oracle of God" (2 Sam. 16:23).

During King David's reign, the seeds of rebellion were being sown.

David's oldest son, Absalom, was a dashing young man with long flowing locks of hair. By misrepresenting himself as a judicial officer at the gates of the city and giving rulings that favored influential people, Absalom amassed power among the Israelites. Soon he formed a vast army and marched toward the Holy City to assassinate his father.

David could not bear to see a battle fought in the streets of Jerusalem, so he and his men fled from the traitors and crossed the brook called Kidron on their way toward the wilderness. David was dismayed when it was confirmed that Ahithophel was counted among the conspirators. He prayed that the Lord would turn the counsel of Ahithophel into foolishness.

As Absalom made his triumphant entry into Jerusalem and usurped his father's authority, Ahithophel accompanied him and quickly took control of the situation. His first recommendation was for Absalom to humiliate David's ten concubines who were left behind at the palace. Next, Ahithophel asked for permission to select 12,000 men to pursue David.

A counselor named Hushai was summoned and Absalom asked for his opinion. Hushai answered that Ahithophel's advice wasn't good at the time because David's warriors were mighty men and were enraged like a bear robbed of her cubs. Hushai went on to suggest that all Israel be gathered together, from Dan to Beersheba, and that Absalom lead them in battle.

The words of Hushai cut to the heart of Absalom. Knowing his father, he became convinced that it would be too dangerous to follow David in hot pursuit. Absalom turned his head slowly and pointed his finger at Ahithophel. "...The counsel of Hushai the Archite is better than the counsel of Ahithophel" (2 Sam. 17:14a).

Those words stung Ahithophel. He knew that his days were numbered. David would become strong again and would destroy the rebellion. Ahithophel slowly turned, saddled his donkey, loaded his stately clothes from the court, and rode the long, dusty journey home. When he arrived at his dwelling place, he put his household in order, wrote his will, and took his life.

The Secret Story

I questioned myself, "What drove this great man to such a hideous death?" After diligently searching the Scriptures, I believe I found the root cause of Ahithophel's failure.

Do you recall the story in the Scriptures of David committing adultery with a woman named Bathsheba? Soon after the act was consummated, Bathsheba discovered that she was pregnant. David ordered Uriah, her husband, to come home from battle. He assumed that Uriah would sleep with Bathsheba, and David could claim that the child she was expecting was not his.

Because his fellow soldiers couldn't leave the battlefield as he did, Uriah, a man of great integrity, retired for the night by the gate of the city, not with his wife. Upon learning this, David had Uriah sent to the front lines of the battle to be killed. The stately counselor who watched this whole affair being played out before him was none other than Ahithophel, Bathsheba's grandfather! (See Second Samuel 11:3; 23:34.)

During Bathsheba's pregnancy, Ahithophel served in David's court, allowing his anger and disgust over David's treatment of his granddaughter to build until it turned to hate.

Was he justified in feeling the way he did about David? Certainly. But instead of trusting God to judge David, he decided to take vengeance into his own hands. People with bitter spirits are attracted to each other. This is why Absalom and Ahithophel became such fast friends and co-conspirators.

If you allow resentment to reside in your heart, you will suddenly find new "friends" who are pulled to you like a magnet. The mutual feelings of bitterness will deepen your own anger.

Ahithophel should have forgiven David, trusting that God would handle the situation.

God was ready to do a wondrous work in Ahithophel's lineage. Bathsheba was not David's first wife; there were others. Legally she had no claim to the throne of Israel. Because of the mercy of God, however, David and Bathsheba's son (Ahithophel's great-grandson) was to become the future king of Israel. Ahithophel's reputation became dishonorable instead of respectable because of the resentment he held within him.

An unforgiving, bitter heart produces an atmosphere for satanic activity.

Entertaining Demons

How would you respond if you discovered someone intended to place an advertisement in your local newspaper that invited demons to enter your house and harass you day and night? Without doubt you would be angry with the initiator and do everything possible to stop the announcement.

Yet, people make such declarations every day. If you allow even the slightest amount of vengeance to linger in your spirit, you are extending an open invitation to satan.

Demon spirits can seriously hamper your efforts to find inner healing and deliverance. For example, if you harbor discontent, before you even realize it, malice can creep in and alter your entire personality. You may think nothing has changed, but those around you will be dismayed by the marked difference in your character. This is why repentance is so vital.

If we close the door to malice, vengeance, bitterness, and anger, satan has far fewer avenues to gain a foothold in our lives. Now, don't read more into this than what I am saying. Just because you are angry today does not mean you will be demon possessed tomorrow, next week, next year, or ever. Demon influence is a result of a slow but methodical process that occurs over a period of months, and even years.

Just as the Lord is patient with us, so is satan. The devil will wait, no matter how long it takes, to deceive you into allowing vengeance to grow into a full-blown force.

When we become emotionally crushed by the death of a loved one, by divorce, or by the loss of employment, it is an opportunity for satan to take unfair advantage. When we cultivate an attitude of self-pity and anger, the door is propped open for any demon spirit to gain entrance.

Satan is a terrorist and uses guerrilla tactics to ensnare you at your most vulnerable moment. Terrorists don't attack military targets that are well protected. Instead, they find defenseless women and children standing in public places or vulnerable situations and kill them.

In the same manner, satan came against the Lord after He had just completed 40 days of fasting in the wilderness of Judea. Jesus had been without nourishment and He was separated from His friends.

The devil challenged Jesus not only once, but three times, poking and probing the gentle Master, endeavoring to discover a weakness in His defenses. Satan realized, though, that Christ would not fall prey to his ploys. The Scriptures relate: "And when the devil had ended all the temptation, he departed from Him *for a season*" (Lk. 4:13). This verse reveals another strategy of satan. He will bide his time until a person he has once tempted is again in a state of weakness.

When I suffered financial loss, my children did also. They too experienced intense, emotional stress. During this painful period, certain people were delivering messages from satan. They came and said things such as, "Your father has an evil spirit and is possessed of the devil. You need to get away from him."

Not only did these words devastate my immediate family members, but when I heard about the lies, it was as though someone stuck a knife in my heart. Then one day I began to comprehend that the events in question were not orchestrated by people, but by demon spirits. That knowledge allowed me to have compassion for my enemies.

The Bible is accurate when it states, "He therefore that despiseth, despiseth not man, but God" (1 Thess. 4:8a).

A Stranglehold

My first encounter with the satanic side of the supernatural began to prepare me for battles I would encounter in seeing the deliverance of hundreds of people controlled by demons.

One day I received a call from a lady in our church asking me to visit her neighbor who was close to death. When I arrived at the home, her nurse met me at the door and quickly ushered me to the woman's bedside. Cancer had taken its toll on her frail body. The thin woman hoarsely addressed me, "Pastor, I don't believe in God, Heaven, or hell, but I thought a prayer wouldn't hurt."

I smiled with understanding at her confusion and reached into my pocket for my New Testament and began reading aloud.

These visits continued on a daily basis for over a month, but then I was called out of town for a weeklong series of services. When I arrived back in New Orleans, there was an urgent message from the nurse awaiting me. I quickly dropped my suitcases off at my house and rushed to the woman's home. The nurse, who was not a believer, led me into the patient's room explaining, "Pastor, it looks like this is it, and she requested that you pray one last time. The cancer has advanced to such a state that at times she goes into uncontrollable fits."

When I turned from the nurse to look at the lady, her body was shaking so violently that it seemed she would fall off the bed. I quickly laid my hand on her feverish brow and exclaimed, "In the name of Jesus I speak healing to this woman's body!" Suddenly, as if on cue, the shaking stopped and her breathing returned to normal. After a few minutes I saw that she was not going to open her eyes and speak, so I left the room.

While I was walking down the hallway, I heard the desperate cry of the nurse calling me back. I rushed back and saw that the woman was once again having convulsions—this time more intensely than before. I repeated my previous prayer and the woman's body lay still. I waited for a longer period of time to observe her, but seeing no change, I again began my exit.

Before I could leave the house, the nurse cried out, "Please don't go; she's doing it again!" When she said those words, the Holy Spirit spoke to my heart: "The woman is not in control. Demons are trying to take her life."

I now understood. What I had thought were the normal signs of death were actually signs of a gigantic struggle between Heaven and hell for the soul of this woman, and I was there to be Heaven's emissary of deliverance.

Entering the room for the third time, I boldly addressed the demon spirits and commanded them to come out of the woman's body. The demons' stranglehold upon the woman was released and she sat up in bed.

Her entire demeanor changed. Looking at me with a smile she said, "Reverend, I believe in God now."

During the next few weeks she began to regain her strength. I learned that her problem started years before when she had become extremely angry with her mother. Her friends invited her to a séance where she might find opportunity for revenge. After numerous encounters with demon spirits in these séances, she finally stopped attending the sessions. The demons, however, continued to haunt her.

Now on her deathbed, she had experienced the power of the only true God and Savior. Jesus broke the demonic oppression. Within a month the woman was completely healed.

Chapter 9

Unexpected Power

The power of God can instantly free you from the influence of satan. But unless you remove what attracted the demons in the first place, your deliverance will be short-lived.

I still remember something that happened in the early part of 1993. I saw the shadow of a man's face as he peered through the glass window of our sanctuary door. An usher invited him in and he found a seat near the rear of the building. The hair of this disheveled man was long and matted together with his beard. He had come to the service with a mixture of drugs and alcohol in his veins.

Later we learned that the man was suffering from extreme depression stemming from a recent divorce, the loss of his children, and the discovery that no one trusted him—including his own family. Although he was only in his early 30's, he looked much older because of the lines of sorrow that were carved into his face.

Suddenly, to the congregation's astonishment, he ran down the aisle in a mad frenzy, pointing in my direction and screaming, "Let me get to him! Let me get to him!"

Just before he reached the spot where I was standing, the power of God grabbed him and slammed him to the floor on his back. I hadn't touched him, nor had any other member of the church. This was a divine act of God and I spontaneously asked the congregation to begin to pray.

At the Name of Jesus, the demons that were inside the man came out. The gentleman stood and turned to face the congregation, a freed man.

The change in his countenance was remarkable. Every person in the building could see the peace of God on his face.

For the next few weeks he attended our church and began cleaning up his life. Soon, however, he decided he no longer needed nor wanted help and the demons returned to seduce him again. He slipped back into the world, carrying his same heavy baggage.

I recently received a call from this man. As I heard his voice coming through the phone, I detected the guttural sound of the same demon I heard at the time of his deliverance.

I sensed that satan had once again wrapped his bitter tentacles around the man's heart and was drawing him into his kingdom of darkness.

I share this story to let you know that instant deliverance does occur, but unless you continue on your path toward God, demons will have access to you again. Total submission to the Lord is required.

Many people become uncomfortable when we talk about supernatural activity, such as with demons and angels. Perhaps it is because we are dealing with the invisible without tangible characteristics that we can see, feel, or touch.

Although it is true that some ministers approach this subject with more hype than reality, that does not diminish the importance of the role of the supernatural in our lives.

Slain in the Spirit

When I was 19 I conducted my first revival at a small country church. I stood behind a rough, oak pulpit and preached the gospel with fervor and faith. Suddenly, while I was preaching, a woman walked slowly to the front of the church. Her left arm and leg were twisted inwardly. I later learned that as a child she had been stricken with polio. The closer she came, the harder I prayed.

By the time she was close enough for me to lay my hands on her, God had already performed a miraculous healing. Her crippled arm and leg were completely normal. When I touched her, she fell backward to the floor, slain in the Spirit. During the remainder of the service, nearly everyone I prayed for fell to the floor under the power of God. I didn't understand what was taking place, since I had neither seen nor heard of anything like this happening. This phenomenon began to occur in most of the revival services that I preached.

Eventually I was approached by church leaders who were uncomfortable with the fact that people were slain in the Spirit and they asked me to discourage it. I did my best to comply with their instructions. Sometimes I even asked people to kneel before I prayed for them so it wouldn't be quite as obvious if they fell.

A Hunger for God

In September, 1965, I was elected as pastor of the First Assembly of God in New Orleans. In my desperation to see revival, I spent much time in fasting and prayer. My hunger for more of God became intense. It brought me into an even deeper relationship with the Lord, until I cried out, "Just give me revival!"

Suddenly the Lord spoke, "Marvin, are you willing to have revival even if, when you pray for people, they fall on the floor and you are criticized?"

My response was, "Yes, Lord, even if they fall." The words stuck in my throat. Although I was intensely praying and felt ready for anything, I had not considered that God might want to rekindle some of the supernatural events I had experienced when I was 19 years old.

At that moment it was as if someone whispered in my ear. The Lord said, "Call Lorne Fox."

"But God, I don't know where to find him," I quickly replied. "He may even be dead by now." I caught myself and repented, "I'm sorry, Lord. If he was dead, You surely wouldn't have asked me to contact him."

Finishing my time of prayer, I felt a release in my spirit, sensing the direction in which God was leading me. I had no idea of the miraculous event that was about to take place.

I drove home to have lunch with my wife and stopped to check the mailbox on my way to the front door. When I pulled open the lid, to my amazement I found a handwritten letter from Lorne Fox! I nervously tore open the envelope and discovered that Brother Fox was not only alive, but that God had been speaking to him about coming to New Orleans to conduct a two-week revival.

With great excitement I returned to my office and dictated a letter suggesting possible dates. I also shared with him the fact that earlier that same day the Lord had instructed me to contact him. I had never been introduced to Lorne Fox, but had seen him from a distance at one of his large crusade meetings.

When I was 17 years old, I watched Brother Fox minister under such a beautiful anointing, and it so impacted me that I still remember the title of his message: "There Was a Man Sent From God, Whose Name Was John."

When he arrived at the church for his first service, the evangelist was dressed in a business suit and was meticulous in his appearance. This refinement could not hide the years that had begun to take their toll on this man of God. His skin was pale and translucent as a result of contracting malaria while on the mission field. His hands trembled slightly and his voice had been weakened by years of speaking, until now he could scarcely be heard above a whisper. A microphone was devised to hang about his neck with a special bracing system that put the microphone's capsule squarely in front of his mouth. None of these devices detracted in any way from the power of this man when he was in the pulpit.

On the first night he preached with such conviction that when he gave a call for those who wished to be healed, a great percentage of people in the packed auditorium came forward for prayer.

Brother Fox motioned for me to come and join him as he began to pray for the sick. When his frail hands reached out to touch the first woman in line, she collapsed to the floor under the power of God. He then turned to me and said, "You pray for the next one." As I reached out my hand to pray for the second lady, she also fell under God's power.

The thought flashed through my mind, "Oh no, it's happening again!" Recovering from my hesitancy, I glanced over to see Brother Fox place his hand on the third person in line, who was also slain in the Spirit. Abruptly he waved his bony arm toward the rest of the people standing in line and exclaimed, "That's it. You're dismissed. The meeting is over and I'll see you tomorrow night."

I was confused and wondered why he would pray for just three people, then close the meeting. He turned to me and said, "I'm not here for them; I'm here for you. Don't worry about the people. They're hungry for God. They will be back."

A Trembling Hand

Brother Fox walked with me to my office. As we were seated, he turned to face me and began his story. "Years ago, when I was a young man, I was carried on a cot to the tent revival of a great evangelist, Charles S. Price. Those who brought me were sure that Dad Price would pray for me and I would be healed, but the service was soon over and he hadn't ministered to me. As he walked through the tent on the way to his car, he stopped next to my cot, turned to me, and said, 'Young man, would you be made whole?' I reached out a trembling hand and as Dad Price spoke the Name of Jesus, strength immediately came into my body like the recharging of a car's dead battery."

Lorne Fox continued, "I was a concert pianist by profession. After my healing that night I immediately offered my services to Charles Price. Soon I was playing the piano for him across the nation. Years later, when Dad Price was dying, he called me to his bedside and said, 'Lorne, the Lord has talked to me and said I am to anoint you and impart the gift of healing from my ministry into yours.' The ministry of healing has continued since that day."

The next night I was overwhelmed by the sight of the massive crowd that had gathered in the building. The ushers were bringing in extra chairs to seat the people. Although the anticipation of the audience was mounting rapidly, it could not match my own expectation after our conversation the previous night. As Brother Fox walked to the podium, a hush fell in the building and hope filled the crowd. We embraced his every word.

From this crusade, Brother Fox's heart and mine were knit together. On another occasion he returned for a second series of meetings. The church had exploded numerically and we were experiencing a great spirit of revival. During this crusade he felt led of the Spirit to share in one of his messages the vision God had given him of Heaven, the cross, and hell. The following is an excerpt from that sermon, which he ministered at First Assembly in New Orleans, on March 4, 1975.

I've had a most remarkable experience, something that is very, very personal. For since the day of that vision until now, there have been seven times when I have met someone and said to myself, "Who are they? I know that person. I've seen them before." And then it dawned on me: I've never seen them on earth, but I saw them in the vision.

The clouds of golden glory are close now. I turned and looked back at someone, and that face was stamped indelibly on my heart.

When I met Brother Gorman the first time I said to myself, "Where have I met you before? I know you like my brother." And I discovered it was real to me. I had seen him in that vision climbing up the hill!

At that moment, Lorne Fox turned toward me and said: "I met you there. We haven't got much further to go, Brother Gorman. For there is a lot to be done in a short time. That, if you want to know, is why I love you so dearly."

I sat on the platform and began to weep as the impact of his words sank into my spirit. I felt humbled that God would be willing to use a man like me.

When I left the meeting that night I was so determined to walk with God that my face was set like a flint and nothing could move it. I knew that if there was a line of people from New Orleans to Chicago and I was forced to walk by and listen to each one of them shouting, "You'll never make it to Heaven!" I would still say unwaveringly as I reached the end of the line, "I'm going to make it in."

A Blue Tie

A few months later the Lord gave me a dream. Our church was packed except for two empty seats on the right side of the auditorium. A man accompanying a blind lady came in and occupied them. In my dream I called the couple forward. I laid hands on her and prayed twice, but with no significant results. As I prayed the third time, the woman's eyes were opened and she touched my chin and said, "You have brown eyes!" I prayed once more and she exclaimed, "What a beautiful blue tie." At this time I was not sure if the dream was symbolic, or if it concerned some actual event that was about to occur.

During the next few services I watched the congregation for such a couple. One Sunday evening we were in the middle of our worship service when a couple caught my attention as they walked down the aisle and sat in the last two empty seats in the auditorium. The gentleman carefully led the lady, who was wearing dark glasses.

The service progressed and, as I was closing my Bible to give the final benediction, the Lord spoke to me: "It's time to pray for the blind lady."

"Lord, I'm not sure she's blind," I argued. I addressed the gentleman, "Sir, is the lady with you blind?"

It was the woman, however, who cried out immediately and pressed her way through the crowd to the front.

"Yes, Brother Gorman. Will you pray for me?" A hush fell over the crowd.

I placed my two thumbs over her eyes and said, "In the Name of Jesus, receive your sight."

As I removed my thumbs she opened her eyes, but she said, "I can't see anything."

I placed my thumbs over her eyelids and prayed again, "Jesus, let this woman receive her sight."

This time when I removed my hands she weakly spoke, "I think I see a speck of light."

The congregation was on the edge of their seats; it was so quiet you could have heard a pin drop. I hesitated for a moment, then felt the gentle nudging of the Lord.

As I had done before, I placed my thumbs over her eyes and prayed for the third time, "In the Name of Jesus, I command you to receive your sight."

When I removed my hands she gasped and reached up with her fingers to touch my chin and said, "You have brown eyes!" I realized, almost in fright, that this was a quote from my dream weeks earlier, and my mind raced wildly as I glanced down to see the color of my tie. Just as in my dream, it was blue! The woman exclaimed, "You have a beautiful blue tie!"

As her voice echoed throughout the sanctuary, the audience broke into ecstatic shouts of joy. My mind was in a whirl. Through my tears I joyfully noticed a prominent member of our church, who was an executive vice president of a large bank in the city. He was falling to his knees and quaking under the power of God, while tears flowed down his face.

Only the power of God operating in the supernatural could bring such release in His people. This special moment reaffirmed to me that God's power, no matter how unusual, should always be embraced.

Chapter 10

A Circle of Love

Tuesday, July 15, 1986, was the most devastating day of my life. That is when I confessed to my wife, Virginia, my infidelity of nearly eight years earlier.

Fear and anxiety overwhelmed me as I summoned the strength to tell her what had happened. I had no idea how she would respond and I was prepared for the worst.

Virginia recalls, "Earlier that afternoon Marvin called to tell me he would have to go to Baton Rouge that night for a meeting with some ministers. I used the time alone to gather some information for our tax return. We had asked for an extension and it would be due the next month."

It was about midnight when I returned from that devastating meeting.

Virginia remembers, "I heard his car in the driveway and I was glad to come downstairs from my office, which was cluttered with the files and receipts I had been organizing."

Immediately, she asked, "How was your trip?"

"Come and sit down with me on the sofa," I said as my heart was breaking. "There are some things I need to tell you."

I told her, "Honey, we are about to face the greatest storm we have ever endured."

My wife looked at me in disbelief as I confessed to her that seven-and-a-half years earlier I had committed an act of adultery. She was in total shock and we both began to weep uncontrollably.

Virginia recalls, "I felt weak. It seemed impossible that this could be happening to me. My whole world seemed to be falling apart. I went into shock. My mouth felt like cotton and I began trembling with chills."

I rushed to the kitchen to get my wife a glass of water. Then we both held each other tightly as we cried together.

After gaining her composure, Virginia began to tell me a story.

She recounted a conversation with the wife of a missionary several months earlier. The woman was encouraging people to write a note to a couple who had gone through the same situation we were now facing. Virginia told the woman, "Oh yes, I'd like to join you and others in writing to them. However, what he did is something I don't think I could ever forgive."

The missionary's wife said something that was totally unexpected. "But, Virginia, you wouldn't have a choice. You'd have to forgive. God forgives."

As we faced that difficult moment, those words rang in Virginia's ears.

Then my wife recalled something else. She took my hands and said, "Honey, do you remember that in his vision, Brother Fox saw you in Heaven? I know God has forgiven you and you will make it to Heaven." Then she held me and continued, "Although I'm devastated, I want you to know I will not leave you. I still love you."

We both cried, searching for words to comfort each other.

Virginia let me know that although she was deeply wounded, our love was secure. As she recalls, "I knew that he was overwhelmed with the fear that I would divorce him. But I assured him that we would face this storm together."

Oh, How It Rained

The next morning, Wednesday, our city was blanketed with a severe thunderstorm and I knew a tempest was also brewing in our church.

We phoned our three children, requesting them and their spouses to come to our house early that morning. When they gathered in our living room, I looked at the rain trickling down the windows and thought, "The sky is weeping along with us."

Randy, my oldest son, was seated beside his wife, Janice. Of course, he was shaken by the news of his father's infidelity, but he tried not to show it. He knew that all have sinned and come short of the glory of God, and was ready to stand by me. We later learned that as they were en route to meet with us Janice had said, "Randy, your dad is planning to resign from the church." Many times God has informed her of impending future events.

When I had finished telling my family, Mark simply stated, "Dad, we knew all along you had feet of clay. But I want you to know we still love and believe in you." He and his wife, Gina, both pledged their continued loyalty.

My daughter, Beverly, and her husband, Garland, at first were unable to speak. Despite the unwelcome news, Garland said, "I don't have any stones to throw."

I was overcome with emotion as each of them expressed their commitment to me as we faced an unknown future. At that moment, I knew I was surrounded by a circle of love.

She Didn't Forget

At approximately 9:30 p.m. that same Wednesday evening, the doorbell rang at our home. It was Mary Helen Bryant, a dear friend of our family. We invited her in and she told us that she had just come from the church service where my resignation was announced. With apology, she said, "Please forgive me for coming without being invited, but I just had to know that the two of you and your children are all right."

Mary Helen was extremely sensitive to what we were going through. A few years earlier she had walked through a similar period of upheaval that led her to our church. She realized that nothing other than the love of Christ could fill the void that was left by the devastating marital problems she had encountered. The moment Mary Helen walked through the doors of our sanctuary, the Lord impressed on her heart, "I know you are here." A few nights later, when the altar call was given, she came forward and gave her heart to the Lord.

Now, seated in our den, she explained that as I prayed with her at the altar of salvation, the Lord spoke to her and said, "One day you will help this man and his family."

At the time, the statement seemed absurd to her because she was in such dire straits spiritually and emotionally. But she never forgot those words.

Mary Helen told us how she listened as the church officials announced the resignation of the man who had been their pastor for more than 20 years. The news hit the congregation like a bomb and they were shell-shocked.

That night, Mary Helen hugged Virginia and said, "You still have the best husband in the world." Then she turned to me, saying, "I've always known you were just a man. But no matter what you have done, Brother Gorman, I forgive you and I still believe in you. I am here to help you and your family."

She was true to her word.

In the months that followed, when we lost everything, she was there. When we needed a car, she bought us one. When there was little food in the house, she would suddenly appear at our backdoor smiling, her arms full of groceries. When there was no money for clothes, she took my wife and bought her apparel from New Orleans' finest department stores. When we lost our home to bankruptcy, she was there to help us move to another location. Her support was much more than material, though. Our spirits were constantly uplifted by her prayers and encouragement.

As a new Christian, Mary Helen had great difficulty understanding how so many who had been ministered to as she had, could turn away so easily without extending love and comfort.

Haunting Thoughts

My wife chose to stay by my side but the deep pain she felt did not quickly subside. As she recalls, "There were days—which ran into weeks—when the thought of Marvin having another woman in his arms haunted me. There are no words to describe my misery. It was a recurring pain that surfaced over and over again." Satan tormented her constantly, reminding her of my failure.

Virginia, however, made a choice. As she says, "I *chose* to forgive and acted on God's Word that declares, 'And be ye kind one to another, tenderhearted, forgiving one another, even as God for Christ's sake hath forgiven you' " (Eph. 4:32).

Virginia did not stop praying. "Every day I sought the face of God and searched the Scriptures, trying to find the answers I needed in order to cope. Healing is a process," she adds. "When a person is deeply wounded by someone they love, they automatically lose the ability to trust. That's how I felt. My trust had been violated."

Before this crisis, Virginia had always been able to totally lean on me, but now that was history. That confidence would have to be restored.

Inwardly, Virginia was weak, but to our family she was like a rock. "I saw the pain Marvin and our children were going through and I felt I could not allow them to see all my grief. I knew they needed me to help them handle their own hurts," she recalled.

Another crisis ran parallel through our lives. Our financial world crumbled and we were enveloped in fear. Says Virginia, "There were nights I wept in bed, hoping he would not notice. Frequently he saw my grief and began to apologize all over again. He felt great shame and was heartsick over what his actions had caused."

Prior to this time, my family saw me as someone who could handle any difficult situation, but this seemed out of my control. If a businessman has a moral failure, usually only a handful of people ever know about it, but because of my public life, I felt the whole world was condemning me. I desperately needed the love of my family.

Virginia and I had enjoyed a wonderful marriage and I placed tremendous confidence in her. Because of what had happened, however, I noticed that things were not the same. As she says, "I knew he could trust me with our children, the checkbook, our music ministry, and other obligations. But during that time I became so discouraged that I lost interest in many things. I didn't care about my weight and put on an extra 12 pounds. I no longer cared about household chores."

I became worried about Virginia's signs of depression. She did not know what the future would hold for our family. "For all my life, I had encouraged people that their strength comes from the Lord," my wife said. "Yet in the time of grief, it was difficult to take heed to my own counsel. But God did not forsake me. In my moments of greatest weakness He was there. He was faithful and I totally depended on Him."

Facing the World Alone

My wife was not a stranger to loneliness. Her first marriage lasted less than two years, when her husband drowned while swimming with his friend. "At the time of his death," she recalls, "I was six-and-one-half months pregnant with my oldest son, Randy. I am acquainted with the sadness of driving myself to the hospital to give birth to my first child."

She also remembers what it was like to sit in a church service with her baby, noticing young couples seated nearby holding hands. "Often I recalled having my husband with me. He sang bass in our church quartet and I accompanied them on the piano. The weekly radio programs would not be the same. He would never be with me again," she said. "I found consolation knowing that one day we will all be reunited in Heaven."

Raising a child without a father seemed to be an overwhelming responsibility to 19-year-old Virginia. "I returned to my job at the bank when Randy was six weeks old. Then, about one year later, the tide turned. I was not to remain a single mom," she remembers.

One night I was speaking at a youth rally when I saw a beautiful young woman enter the sanctuary, carrying her son. I was astounded when God spoke to me and said, "She will be your wife."

After a five-month courtship, we both knew that we were deeply in love and that the Lord had ordained us to be united as husband and wife, to spend the rest of our lives together.

When the scope of our ministry began to grow, there were many days and nights Virginia had to remain at home with the children. "Often, I felt like a martyr," she recalls. "I thought the congregation should be proud of me for accomplishing the tasks of feeding, dressing, and driving my children to the services, with my husband ministering miles away."

When we moved to New Orleans and my duties began to increase, the time I was able to spend with my family became less and less. "I selfishly resented having to share Marvin with others," Virginia said. "I became jealous of his schedule and longed for quality and quantity time that the five us of could spend together as a family."

I am not recommending that people experience a crisis to bring a family closer together, but that is exactly what happened in our home. That's why I tell people everywhere to cherish every moment you can spend with those you love. Don't allow anything to pull you apart.

Virginia was recently talking about our valley of despair, and here are her observations:

The crisis our family endured has enlightened me in many ways. God has shown me that often women who are unhappy in their marriage go to church seeking to find peace. Many of them have been mistreated, abused, and made to feel that they are a failure. They look at a minister who is dressed nicely in his suit and tie, smiling and giving his best effort to encourage the people of his congregation. However, he may be encountering tremendous difficulties in his own life, perhaps with a wife who has no burden for the ministry, wayward children, financial struggles, sickness, or other problems. Yet a good pastor will put aside his own problems and zero in on the needs of the people in the pews.

Because they see his compassionate nature, it often becomes difficult for someone to differentiate between the godly love of a minister and the love she craves from her own companion. There are times when a female looks at her minister as being more than her spiritual leader. Her imagination runs rampant. The devil begins to influence her. She thinks how wonderful it would be if she could be with him instead of with her own husband. She fantasizes that the world would be bliss with him, so she pursues a relationship. Satan wants to set a trap for both parties, her and the minister.

I have always known that Marvin never loved anyone but me. However, if that story were different, God would have still given me the ability to forgive. No matter what situation a person faces, God will give grace to cope with it and to be an overcomer.

When I faced my crisis in July, 1986, I had no intention of leaving Marvin. However, there were times when that thought crossed my mind. It might be easier to ignore the anger and hurt if we were apart. Maybe then I wouldn't have to deal with it all, I reasoned.

Marvin had admitted to what he did wrong. There were many false accusations and it seemed to be too much for me to handle. I knew I could get a job to support myself. I could just throw in the towel and forget it. Then I wouldn't have to face the people who were upset with him. It seemed to make sense. I could just move to another city and start over. However, those thoughts were not coming from the Lord, but from my deep hurts. That was not God's will.

I felt a strong allegiance to the Body of Christ. If I divorced my husband, what would happen to my testimony? How many people would lose confidence in the Lord? We had always believed and taught that God forgives and brings peace. I sincerely did not want to cause people to turn away from the Lord. If He couldn't heal our marriage, how could they expect Him to heal theirs?

Another factor was that I didn't want to bring division with our children. They might have to choose which one of us they would remain close to. I wanted them to love and respect both their father and me. God caused me to realize that it was a trick of the enemy for me to even consider a divorce. In fact, I would have been a fool to leave a loving husband and father. Oh, the road was a little bumpy at times, but we held on tight and kept praying and working at it.

There is no doubt in my mind that I made the right decision. I'm very thankful that I remained in my marriage. Marvin and I are closer to each other now than we have ever been. Our prayer is that we can influence other couples to become more devoted to each other. We are in marriage "For better, for worse, for richer, for poorer; in sickness and in health, till death do us part."

Risking Her Life

It is impossible to place a value on the impact of just one loyal friend who is there at a time of need.

One day, as I was reading the Old Testament, the Holy Spirit led me to the story of a woman named Rizpah.

After Saul's death, the judgment of God fell upon two of his sons and five of his grandsons (see 2 Sam. 21:1-14). Israel was experiencing the third year of a drastic drought, for Saul had slaughtered the Gibeonites when he was commanded by God to be their protector. In retribution for Saul's sin, the Gibeonites asked for seven of his descendants to be delivered to them so they could hang them on a hill.

When Rizpah, a concubine of Saul and the mother of two of his sons, heard of their death, she raced through the moonlit night toward the place of their punishment. Though her family members were dead, she could not bear for them to be mocked any further. She chose to risk her life so she could protect their bodies from the birds and beasts.

As dawn was breaking, Rizpah took sackcloth, spread it upon a rock, and covered them. In the time of famine, through blistering heat and frigid nights, she beat back vultures and wild animals that would destroy their bodies.

The news of this woman's dedication reached the palace of King David. He was so moved by her actions that he assembled his men to retrieve the bones of Saul and Jonathan, as well as the bodies of those Rizpah had been protecting. They were all buried with honor in the grave of Kish, the father of Saul.

The Lord was pleased by this woman's act of compassion and David's dedication to Saul. The drought was broken, and water once again flowed freely in the land.

The compassion of a true friend is a gift to be cherished. The apostle Paul said that in Christ we are part of God's "family in heaven and earth" (Eph. 3:15).

I know we could not have weathered the storm without the people who gave us their love. The relatives on both sides of our family—my wife's and mine—stood by us.

After confessing to my wife, our children and their spouses, I faced a most difficult task. How was I going to explain my failure to my mother, whom I also loved deeply. She had always been there for me. Virginia and I drove the 400-mile trip to Hampton, Arkansas, where I related the story I know she would rather not have heard. Once again I felt the same genuine love and support I remembered receiving from her as a child. Now the *circle of love* had widened to include my mother. It was critical to me at that time to have the support of my entire family.

Only the Lord knows what it meant to us to have loyal friends who contacted us regularly and ministered love and encouragement. The following friends are some of those who consistently reached out to minister healing to us.

Johnny and Gloria Cherry and their children always kept in touch. We enjoyed great times of fellowship in their home as well as in ours. They phoned us almost daily during the first few years. They always remembered us with fresh vegetables from Brother Cherry's garden, and with delicious Louisiana shrimp when he had a successful shrimping season. Even though their loyalty caused them to lose friends and to experience rejection by some they had served with for many years, they never wavered in their efforts to restore and befriend us.

Owen Carr and I have been close for many years. We spent much time together while ministering as a team at camp meetings and various Assemblies of God district meetings. We shared precious prayer times and felt comfortable with opening our hearts to each other regarding spiritual matters. Owen and Priscilla's friendship remained constant during our storm. He frequently wrote and phoned us. Occasionally he included a check with his letter, which was very helpful during those lean years following my resignation from the church. On several occasions Owen and Priscilla visited us, even though he ran the risk of jeopardizing his credentials with the Assemblies of God.

No person called me more often, and caused me to laugh more, than Gene Jackson. I looked forward to his calls because of his positive outlook, encouragement, and lightheartedness. Gene and Janet welcomed us to stay in their home. They also drove to New Orleans and spent time in our home. They were criticized, but stood firmly with us as true friends.

Everyone who knows Karl and Joyce Strader are well aware of their love and friendship to the Body of Christ, and more especially to those who are hurting. Their phone calls and Joyce's cards and letters were a continuous source of encouragement and comfort to our entire family. Karl was used mightily in helping our son, Mark, during some of his most difficult days following my resignation. We will always treasure the memories of their loving concern.

Howard and Vestal Goodman and their children stood by us from the moment our crisis began. Immediately following my resignation, they, along with Mike Murdock, Ron Dryden, and Big John Hall, flew to New Orleans at their own expense and worked with our children on our national telecasts. We could never convey how their ministry comforted us and their moral support strengthened us during those dark days.

There are many others whose loving concern was so meaningful to me and my family. The ones mentioned above are the ones who stepped forth immediately, but over the years there were many, too numerous to name, who contributed greatly to our restoration.

Jonathan's Covenant

Do you remember the story of how Jonathan befriended David, even at the risk of losing his future throne? As a young man, Jonathan had a deep spiritual perception about the importance of God's destiny for his life.

At that time David had just killed Goliath, and the congratulations of King Saul were ringing in his ears.

Jonathan, Saul's firstborn son and heir to the throne, could have become jealous of David's acclaim. Instead, he was devoted to David, made a covenant with him, and "loved him as his own soul" (1 Sam. 18:1). At one point, Jonathan took off his princely robe, armor, sword, and belt and placed them on David. With that symbolic act he gave up his spiritual right to the throne.

As the months and years progressed, Saul became increasingly jealous of David, finally screaming at his son Jonathan, asking that he and the servants kill David. Saul later attempted to pin David to the wall. Even these rash actions could not shake Jonathan's faith in David.

David responded with deep sorrow when he found that Saul and Jonathan had been killed in battle. Even though he had been a target of King Saul for years and was forced to live as a fugitive, David felt that the two of them were like family to him. There were times when Saul deeply hurt him, but David continued to show him love. When Saul and Jonathan died, David led all of Israel into mourning.

David sang:

The beauty of Israel is slain upon thy high places: how are the mighty fallen! (2 Samuel 1:19)

Saul and Jonathan were lovely and pleasant in their lives, and in their death they were not divided: they were swifter than eagles, they were stronger than lions (2 Samuel 1:23).

As I think about David and Jonathan, I pray that Christians everywhere will demonstrate their love and' compassion to members of the Body of Christ who have fallen.

Recently I spoke with Jim Bakker, the former head of PTL, whose ministry was shattered and who was sentenced to a federal penitentiary. He told me about C.M. Ward, one of the stalwart greats of the Assemblies of God denomination who preached for 25 years on their weekly national radio program, "Revivaltime." Jim said that each month while he was in prison, C.M. Ward wrote to him faithfully and sent him a gift of $25 to provide for his essentials.

An immediate response to a person who makes a mistake often sets the tone for the entire healing process.

I can tell you from personal experience that one of the deepest fears a person has, who has been discovered in a transgression, is that no one will ever believe in him again. An expression of your loyalty and love to that person becomes crucial and should be made as soon as you hear about the problem.

Oh, how I pray that those who are facing a personal trial will have family and friends as strong as mine.

Remember, when you reach out to someone, you are not condoning behavior that is wrong. God will handle the department of justice. He wants us to handle the administration of healing.

As a Christian, look around you. Do you see someone who is hurting? Embrace him or her with love and compassion.

Her Name Was Cindy

One Sunday morning while I was preaching, I noticed a teenage girl seated near the back of our auditorium. She was hanging on every word of my sermon. I could see the spiritual hunger written on her young face. I intended to introduce myself to her after the service, but she slipped out before I could make my way to where she was seated.

The following Wednesday evening she returned. When the invitation was given at the close of the message, she responded and accepted Jesus into her heart. I spoke to her for a few minutes at the altar. Her name was Cindy, but she would not volunteer her last name nor give us much information.

The next Sunday morning Cindy returned. With her was a young girl about ten years old. After I ministered the Word, they both came forward during the altar service. Cindy, not knowing exactly how to express it, said, "Brother Gorman, this is my little sister, Debbie.

Will you put Jesus in her heart like you put Him in my heart?" We prayed together and they left the building.

During the following week I couldn't seem to get the faces of those two young girls out of my mind. I continually asked the Lord to bless them and keep them in His care.

Just as I had hoped, they were present again the next Sunday morning. Seated between them was a little boy, who looked to be around five years of age. As I preached, I could see them whispering. I assumed they were explaining my sermon to him. When the salvation call was given, they came forward holding hands. Cindy said, "Brother Gorman, this is our little brother, Johnny. Will you put Jesus in his heart like you did mine and Debbie's?"

I prayed with Johnny and he asked Christ into his young life.

After ministering to several more people at the altar, I began to walk toward the back of the auditorium. To my dismay, the three children were already gone. I spoke with several members of our congregation and no one seemed to know anything about these young people. "Lord, please let them return," I prayed.

The next Sunday they were back and I was able to speak with them. I told Cindy that some of our church ladies would like to visit their home and meet their parents. Cindy explained that she did not want anyone to visit because their mother was a prostitute.

A Lesson in Love

One morning I greeted Cindy as she was coming into the church. I reached out to touch her arm as I spoke to her. She grimaced with pain and pulled away. I asked, "Is there anything wrong?"

The young girl looked to the floor and responded, "Oh, nothing."

After the service I asked my wife and another lady to take Cindy into the ladies' room to see if there might be something wrong with her arm or back. In a few minutes my wife, Virginia, brought the girl with her to my office. She explained, with tears in her eyes, that Cindy had been beaten so badly that her undergarments were sticking to her back.

The moment I heard those words, anger rose within me like a volcano. I said, "Cindy, we will hire an attorney immediately and begin proceedings to find a new home for you and your sister and brother." I even suggested that we would like to have them stay with us for awhile.

Cindy began to cry, "But Brother Gorman, you don't understand."

"Yes, I do understand!" I told her. "You need to be taken out of that home. You, Debbie, and Johnny need to be free from this kind of treatment. You deserve to be living with a Christian family, so that you can be cared for properly," I explained.

Cindy pleaded again, "But you don't understand. If we stay with our mom, I will always remember to pray for her. If we leave, I might forget how much she needs Jesus."

All I could do was sit back in my office chair and wipe away the tears. This young lady had just preached to me the greatest story I had ever heard on love! She had an understanding of God's divine purpose, no matter what the cost!

Chapter 11

New Wings for Flying

Larry was a top salesman for one of the area's leading automobile dealerships. His family, however, did not enjoy the benefits of his high income. Satan enticed him into gambling and other vices that consumed the rewards of his labor.

I remember the Saturday morning Larry came to my church office at the invitation of a former gambling buddy. He was at his lowest ebb. His marriage was on the rocks, he was deeply in debt from gambling, and he had problems with drug use. The difficulties he faced were causing him to contemplate suicide.

The Lord enabled me to exercise the authority of the Name of Jesus in casting out demons that were attacking his life. Larry was totally transformed. Not long after his conversion, he was promoted to General Sales Manager at a large automobile firm. It became the number one Lincoln-Mercury dealership in an eight-state area and Larry gave God the glory for his success. He became a faithful tither to the church and was a generous supporter of our television ministry.

Before long Larry bought his own automobile dealership in a nearby city. Out of gratitude to God for His blessings and because of Larry's love for me and my family, he furnished us with a new automobile each year.

Unfortunately, Larry's business and marriage started to fail about the time that my storm began. Within a year, he stopped attending church, and eventually lost his marriage and his automobile dealership.

In the confusion of those days, many erroneous stories were told to Larry, which led him to believe that I was obsessed with anger and did not wish to see any of my former church members.

When he finally got the courage to call me, and I reaffirmed my concern for him and assured him of God's love, he began to see things in a different light.

I recently had lunch at a Chinese restaurant which Larry now manages. Together we will work until the relationship we previously shared is fully restored.

Going Separate Ways

It's easy to allow the events of our lives to become a wedge that can destroy a relationship.

Abraham, the father of Israel, was called "a friend of God." He also had a great alliance with his nephew, Lot. At one period in their lives, however, their herdsmen began bickering with each other regarding a boundary line. The contention became so great that the two men separated from each other. Abraham went into the high plains and Lot chose the area near the city of Sodom.

Lot's life took a terrible turn. His relationship with God had depended upon his association with Abraham. Since Abraham's residence was no longer near Lot's home, God seemed even more distant. It was only through the intercession of Abraham and a later visitation by an angel of the Lord that Lot's life was spared from total destruction.

Many times we lean on church leaders so heavily that when they are shaken, we become discouraged. Many members of my former pastorate in New Orleans were affected in this manner. In recent days, however, I have rejoiced to see many people returning to a closeness with the Lord. Now they are not dependent on me, but are riveted in righteousness to the Rock, Christ Jesus.

The Message

When you are in the midst of chaos, the Lord always seems to have a surprise in store. Often He sends people whom you have never met to encourage you.

One evening I was sitting with my family and friends in a back dining room of a Denny's Restaurant in a suburb of New Orleans. A stranger walked through the doorway of our private dining room, came over to me, and said, "Brother Gorman, if you have never believed in divine guidance, you will after this. I had a difficult time finding you. I went to your former church and they were not sure how you could be located. Then God told me where you were."

I didn't say a word, but listened as the man continued. "You see, Brother Gorman, God sent me many miles to deliver a message to you. The Lord told me to tell you that you have a pure heart and He loves you very much. He is going to restore you, and your ministry will be greater in the end than it was in the beginning. God also told me to be your friend." The man then turned around and walked out the door.

To be honest, I thought the fellow was a bona fide quack. I had received so many "words" from people—most of them negative—that I found it hard to take this gentleman seriously.

One month later I received a call on my unlisted phone line from a man who identified himself as Paul Cain. I neither recognized the name, nor made the connection that he was the man who had spoken to me at Denny's. He repeated the same words of encouragement. He continued to call me every four to six weeks throughout the next year.

I later learned that Paul Cain's finding me at the restaurant was even more dramatic than I had originally perceived. When he was driving around searching, the Lord told him that I was in a Denny's Restaurant which was near a Shoney's Restaurant. He inquired of a service station attendant and was directed to the right place. As he entered he saw only a few people, so he returned to his car. God spoke to him again, "Marvin is in there. Go back inside!" Paul reentered the restaurant and asked a waitress if there were any church people eating there. She said, "Oh, yes, there are several in that back dining room."

I Hung Up

The next year in January, 1988, on a crystal-clear Saturday morning, I was startled to again hear the voice of Paul Cain. He began to tell me things that he had seen in the Spirit about Jimmy Swaggart. He saw newsmen with television cameras and a breaking story about Jimmy. I know from the questions he asked me that day, He had greater knowledge than he indicated to me. (This was one-and-a-half months before Jimmy's fall was known publicly.)

As Brother Cain conversed with me, he described events that I knew were relatively unknown. I only knew of four people who were aware of these facts. Paul was so knowledgeable about these events that it frightened me, so I chastised him and hung up the phone. When he immediately called back, I decided to let him talk to my answering machine.

The recorder beeped and Paul said, "Brother Gorman, I don't want to hurt you or your family. You have already been hurt enough. God has shown me some things concerning Jimmy Swaggart and I confronted him. I thought you could shed some light on the events. God told me to be friends with both Jimmy and you. (Paul later told me it did not work out that way on the part of Jimmy.) I know you are probably standing there listening to me right now. I don't expect you to pick up the phone and talk to me again. However, I just want you to know I'm sorry for offending you a few minutes ago. I love you and want to be your friend."

During the next six weeks, every time I prayed, whether day or night, Paul Cain's name appeared clearly before me. It was like a neon sign with blue letters. I began to feel so condemned for the way I had treated him that I finally decided to attempt to locate this man called Paul Cain and plead for his forgiveness.

After making several phone calls to various ministries, my secretary obtained his home phone number in Phoenix, Arizona. We made numerous calls over a period of three or four weeks, but to no avail.

One day my sister-in-law, Ella Gorman, phoned to ask if I knew a prophet by the name of Paul Cain. Her pastor had scheduled him to minister at their church in Kilgore,

Texas. As a result of that conversation I spoke with her pastor and obtained Paul's correct phone number.

When he answered the phone I quickly apologized, "I'm sorry for the way I spoke to you a number of weeks ago, and for slamming down the receiver."

"It's okay, Brother Gorman. It did hurt me, but I forgive you," he replied.

"Paul, I need to see you," I stated. "God told me that I have to sit down in person and talk with you. Apologizing to you by phone is not sufficient."

"Why don't you go to Kansas City with me?" he asked. "I will be speaking at a conference there."

"I am very sorry, but I can't. I have gone through bankruptcy, and I honestly can't afford to come."

"I'll pay your expenses. I will call you back in a few minutes and tell you which airline you will be flying."

When I arrived in Kansas City, I was met at the airport by Paul Cain and Mike Bickle, the pastor of Vineyard Fellowship in Kansas City. When I saw Paul I was stunned. I remarked, "I know you. I've seen you before."

"Yes, I was the one at the Denny's Restaurant."

A Visitation

Months after this meeting with Paul, a gentleman walked into our church in Metairie. He was employed with American Airlines and had flown to our city specifically to deliver a message of encouragement. He proceeded to give me the same message that Brother Cain had, almost word for word.

The Scriptures tell us, "...in the mouth of two or three witnesses every word may be established" (Mt. 18:16). No matter how heavy your load may become, Jesus will be right there.

Your visitations of encouragement may not be as dramatic as mine, but even a Scripture given to you by the smallest child could be the strength you desperately need. Elijah the prophet found himself in the wilderness, being ministered to by ravens. Though ravens are not as majestic as eagles, their message to Elijah was still one of comfort.

In the days ahead, as the Church matures to its full stature in Christ, more and more Christians will realize their need to strengthen and encourage the wounded.

Brand-new Wings

The American eagle is one of the most magnificent birds in the world. Even this symbol of America's greatness at times goes through periods of personal suffering and degradation. The process I'm referring to is called *molting*. The eagle will fly to some lonely spot and there, in absolute solitude, his feathers will begin to flutter to the ground. The molting process gives this majestic bird an unsightly appearance.

During this period, when the bird has no ability to hunt for himself, the eagle is extremely vulnerable to the elements and other hazards that could bring death. At this time other healthy, fully-feathered eagles will fly to the place where the defenseless lone eagle lies and minister to him with nourishment.

Those who study nature have discovered a peculiar fact concerning molting. The only eagle that will feed another fellow eagle in his interval of isolation is one that has also gone through the same process. Soon the separated eagle, which was fed by his friends, regains his feathers, rises from his nest of despair, and stretches out his wings beneath the sun. An eagle's healing is in his wings, which mount up and soar high above the storms once again.

God's message to the hurting has not changed: "But they that wait upon the Lord shall renew their strength; they shall mount up with wings as eagles; they shall run, and not be weary; and they shall walk, and not faint" (Is. 40:31).

I am grateful to God that through our relationship with Jesus Christ and His sufferings, He causes us to be sensitive to the pain of others. By bringing healing, we *find* healing. It is part of God's process of giving us new wings for flying.

Chapter 12

"You Shall Not Die!"

Perhaps the greatest barrier to the process of inner healing is identifying the real problem. So often we zero in on one target and feel we have found the cause, only to discover that the problem resurfaces in other places. Or we may ask forgiveness of someone else, yet never truly forgive ourselves.

On the road to repentance we will identify issues that need to be corrected. However, the obstructions we see often blind our view.

There is a marvelous story in God's Word that speaks to this issue. I realize that I have referred to it previously. However, it so aptly portrays what I am trying to say at this point that I feel it should be repeated, with more detail.

King David's kingdom was prospering, he was secure on his throne, and Israel had gained a reputation throughout the world as a strong nation. Then one afternoon while David was relaxing at the palace, he wandered onto his rooftop patio to gaze out over his city. His idle mind caught a glimpse of Bathsheba bathing and he was so intrigued by her beauty that he sent for her. When she arrived, they met alone and were soon lost in an act of passion. David knew what he had done was wrong, but felt since he was king, he was above reproach. In truth, committing adultery was the result of a much deeper problem that David himself was not aware of at that time. It was not until David began to work his way through *true repentance*, as discussed in Psalm 51, that he began to see and understand the hidden iniquities in his own heart.

A short time later, Bathsheba came running to David's palace with the alarming news that she was pregnant. Her husband, Uriah, was still at the battlefront with Joab and David's powerful army. They were not expected to return for at least a year.

David realized he must act quickly. He sent one of his fastest messengers to the scene of the battle with instructions for Joab to have Uriah returned to his family. When Uriah arrived, however, he had such integrity that he felt it was wrong to sleep with his wife when his fellow soldiers were still at war. Instead, he waited at the gate of the city for King David's message regarding when he could return to his men. This further complicated David's situation.

Before the break of dawn, David conceived a devilish plot and proceeded to pen a note to his general, Joab. It simply said, "Set ye Uriah in the forefront of the hottest battle, and retire ye from him, that he may be smitten, and die" (2 Sam. 11:15). David then reached for the candle and dripped hot wax upon the parchment, sealing it from the eyes of Uriah. He pressed his signet ring into the cooling paraffin, leaving the imprint of the star of David designed from his signature in Hebrew.

An Unexpected Visit

The rising sun awakened the sleeping Uriah at the gate. A messenger handed him the letter, and soon Uriah was off to the battlefield carrying the message that sealed his own death. Within days the deed was done and Bathsheba went into mourning while David made hasty wedding plans. A short time later, the couple was married and David felt that all his problems were behind him. In reality, however, he had simply added another layer of troubles on top of deeper problems that had been there all along.

As the time approached for the child's birth, David received an unexpected visit from Nathan, the prophet. Nathan walked into David's majestic council chambers and said, "I have a parable to tell you." He began, "...There were two men in one city; the one rich, and the other poor. The rich man had exceeding many flocks and herds: but the poor man had nothing, save one little ewe lamb, which he had bought and nourished up: and it grew up together with him, and with his children; it did eat of his own meat, and drank of his own cup, and lay in his bosom, and was unto him as a daughter" (2 Sam. 12:1-3).

Nathan continued, "And there came a traveller unto the rich man, and he spared to take of his own flock and of his own herd, to dress for the wayfaring man that was come unto him; but took the poor man's lamb, and dressed it for the man that was come to him" (2 Sam. 12:4). The cherished family pet had been slaughtered by the selfish neighbor.

After listening intently, David suddenly flew into a rage. I can almost envision in my mind's eye that his golden scepter fell clanging to the floor, as he tore his own robe from his body and threw it upon the polished marble. While Nathan was telling the story, perhaps the king's mind flashed back to the time he had been just a shepherd boy himself and had cuddled his own lambs out on the hillside. It was in those moments of tenderness that David wrote some of his most profound songs, such as, "The Lord is my shepherd; I shall not want" (Ps. 23:1). What outrage to consider that a man in his own kingdom would have no respect for his poor neighbor's small lamb! David gathered his thoughts and in a kingly fashion declared, "...As the Lord liveth, the man that hath done this thing shall surely die: and he shall restore the lamb fourfold, because he did this thing, and because he had no pity" (2 Sam. 12:5-6).

The Lesson

Nathan was a prophet who knew how to work silence to an advantage, and he waited quietly. When the enraged king sat down, and silence once again controlled the room, Nathan raised his head, looked David squarely in the face, and spoke with a voice that pierced the air. "Thou art the man."

...Thus saith the Lord God of Israel, I anointed thee king over Israel, and I delivered thee out of the hand of Saul; and I gave thee thy master's house, and thy master's wives into thy bosom, and gave thee the house of Israel and of Judah; and if that had been too little, I would moreover have given unto thee such and such things. Wherefore hast thou despised the commandment of the Lord, to do evil in His sight? thou hast killed Uriah the Hittite with the sword, and hast taken his wife to be thy wife, and hast slain him with the sword of the children of Ammon. Now therefore the sword shall never depart from thine house; because thou hast despised Me, and hast taken the wife of Uriah the Hittite to be thy wife. Thus saith the Lord, Behold, I will raise up evil against thee out of thine own house, and I will take thy wives before thine eyes, and give them unto thy neighbour, and he shall lie

with thy wives in the sight of this sun. For thou didst it secretly: but I will do this thing before all Israel, and before the sun. And David said unto Nathan, I have sinned against the Lord. And Nathan said unto David, The Lord also hath put away thy sin; thou shalt not die. Howbeit, because by this deed thou hast given great occasion to the enemies of the Lord to blaspheme, the child also that is born unto thee shall surely die (2 Samuel 12:7-14).

The Lord, through this prophecy, was not just punishing David for his sin, but was sending him through a process of inner healing that would divulge deeper issues in his personal life, his family, and the whole nation of Israel. We are still learning from his experience today!

As the years progressed David had to deal with incest, murder, and finally, dethroning by his rebellious son, Absalom. Not all of us will wrestle with the levels of difficulty David faced. When God chose him to be king, He already knew that David would commit adultery. Remember, God knew you when you were in your mother's womb and He knew situations would arise in your life, but He still joyfully chose you!

A Powerful Song

The Scriptures clearly show us that David received complete inner healing, and he chronicles this process in what many believe is his most powerful song. David, realizing the disaster of adultery and murder and their languishing effects on his family, penned these words in his fifty-first Psalm.

I ask you to read it carefully as it reveals his spirit of repentance.

Have mercy upon me, O God, according to Thy lovingkindness: according unto the multitude of Thy tender mercies blot out my transgressions. Wash me throughly from mine iniquity, and cleanse me from my sin. For I acknowledge my transgressions: and my sin is ever before me. Against Thee, Thee only, have I sinned, and done this evil in Thy sight: that Thou mightest be justified when Thou speakest, and be clear when Thou judgest. Behold, I was shapen in iniquity, and in sin did my mother conceive me. Behold, Thou desirest truth in the inward parts: and in the hidden part Thou shalt make me to know wisdom. Purge me with hyssop, and I shall be clean: wash me, and I shall be whiter than snow. Make me to hear joy and gladness; that the bones which Thou hast broken may rejoice. Hide Thy face from my sins, and blot out all mine iniquities. Create in me a clean heart, O God; and renew a right spirit within me. Cast me not away from Thy presence; and take not thy holy spirit from me. Restore unto me the joy of Thy salvation; and uphold me with thy free spirit. Then will I teach transgressors Thy ways; and sinners shall be converted unto

Thee. Deliver me from bloodguiltiness, O God, Thou God of my salvation: and my tongue shall sing aloud of Thy righteousness. O Lord, open Thou my lips; and my mouth shall shew forth Thy praise. For Thou desirest not sacrifice; else would I give it: Thou delightest not in burnt offering. The sacrifices of God are a broken spirit: a broken and a contrite heart, O God, Thou wilt not despise. Do good in Thy good pleasure unto Zion: build Thou the walls of Jerusalem. Then shalt Thou be pleased with the sacrifices of righteousness, with burnt offering and whole burnt offering: then shall they offer bullocks upon Thine altar (Psalm 51).

David had a clear understanding of his sin against God. He was not struggling with the vengeance of others; he was battling with the reprisal of God. The clarity of his appeal produces the perfection of which the apostle John in the New Testament writes concerning the Book of Revelation, calling it the "key of David" (see Rev. 3:7).

God's plan for your future is restoration, not rebellion; peace, not punishment; healing, not heartache; forgiveness, not fear. He wants you to live and not die.

Chapter 13

The Healing

When my life seemed to be plummeting out of control, I wrestled with this question: Why did I fall so easily into sin when I was faced with the opportunity to commit sexual infidelity on that one particular day?

The inner turmoil and confusion that followed my transgression pulled me in many directions. At first I thought the sin of adultery was my major problem, but I knew that sexual immorality had never been part of my nature. I knew that I deeply loved my wife and had found complete happiness in our relationship. Feeling lust for other women was not an area of weakness or temptation to me!

My moment of infidelity came as a completely surprising, spontaneous event. It was not something I had been plotting. When it happened, it was a total shock to me!

In my time alone with God, He began to show me why I had been so vulnerable, why I had crossed the line. I realized that my first step to failure was in neglecting to care for my own spiritual vineyard. I had become so busy doing the *work* of God that I hadn't spent enough *time* with God. As a pastor with hundreds of responsibilities, I allowed my life to become so crowded that I did not walk with Him "in the cool of the day." This lack of personal time for meditation and prayer had weakened my defenses.

Next, the Lord showed me I had somehow convinced myself that "people needed me." That was a lie. They didn't need *me*; they needed a relationship with Jesus Christ. This perception of "being needed" is a stumbling block common to many church leaders. It flatters our ego to think that the Kingdom of God could not possibly move forward without our action or approval. I was lulled into a false sense of security, believing I was indispensable.

Failing Myself

The issues of "lack of prayer" and "being needed" were only part of the puzzle. I also struggled with the question of forgiveness. I knew my act of adultery was wrong, and I knew God had forgiven me the moment I first repented. The problem that plagued me, however, was an inability to forgive myself. There seemed to be a never-ending cycle that produced more self-anger, which was released in my frustration toward others.

Confessing your sins to the Lord will bring peace between you and God, but it does not necessarily release you from personal condemnation. During this period of my life I had difficulty sustaining my own self-worth. Not only had I failed God, my family, the church, and my friends, but I had also failed myself.

When Jesus was asked, "Master, which is the great commandment in the law?" (Mt. 22:36), He replied, "...Thou shalt love the Lord thy God with all thy heart, and with all thy soul, and with all thy mind. This is the first and great commandment. And the second is like unto it, Thou shalt love thy neighbour as thyself" (Mt. 22:37-39).

Christ was saying that if we don't love ourselves, it is impossible to truly love others. He was not talking about an inflated ego or pride, but a healthy regard and esteem of our own worth.

It is easy to identify those who do not properly respect and love themselves. They often compensate for their inferiority and the pain of their low self-esteem by turning their wrath outward. They blame others for their problems, and are perceived as arrogant and proud.

My lack of self-worth drove me to search for answers. Yet the more I grasped for the elusive satisfaction of complete forgiveness, the more frustrated and angry I became with myself. I knew there was something still missing.

In the days just before my sin became known, my ministry seemed more secure than it had ever been. To any observer, there was no indication that anything was amiss, but deep within me was an insecurity that was like a boiling cauldron. I constantly worried that my secret might one day become known. This generated a constant sense of insecurity and low self-esteem.

The Lesson of a Fisherman

What happened when my sin was exposed? There was a feeling of total relief when I realized that the hiding was over. Now everyone knew. Yet my insecurity not only continued, but became even more acute.

You can be forgiven of a sin by God, but that doesn't mean you have been able to forgive yourself. The apostle Peter is a good example of this truth. Just before Jesus was judged by Pilate and the high priest, Peter was found in the courtyard warming himself near an open fire. Three times he was accused of being a follower of Jesus Christ and three times he denied ever knowing the Lord (see Mk. 14:66-72).

After the third denial, as dawn began to break, a rooster crowed to usher in the new day. When the cock's sound cackled through the crisp morning air, the words of Jesus haunted him: "...Verily I say unto thee, That this day, even in this night, before the cock crow twice, thou shalt deny Me thrice" (Mk. 14:30).

Peter dashed out of the courtyard weeping bitterly until he received forgiveness from the Lord. God pardoned him, but Peter couldn't forgive himself. That is why he went back to fishing even after Jesus rose again. Peter still thought he was not worthy to fulfill the call that Jesus had placed upon him. When Christ appeared unto the disciples He asked Peter, "...lovest thou Me more than these? He saith unto Him, Yea, Lord; Thou knowest that I love Thee..." (Jn. 21:15).

He asked Peter the same question three times and each time Peter became more exasperated with the Lord's questioning. Jesus was showing Peter that true self-worth is only found in loving the Lord without reservation.

When we realize our value to Christ, it changes the way we feel about ourselves. His acceptance far outweighs that of any other person. As the apostle Paul said, "But he that glorieth, let him glory in the Lord" (2 Cor. 10:17).

There is no replacement for self-assurance that is built on the Rock, Christ Jesus. The self-esteem I am discussing cannot be obtained without a consistent prayer life. Prayer is the glue that cements your relationship with Jesus. Without this bonding process, your self-worth can be dislodged again and again. That is why I advise Christians everywhere to make an hour of prayer a permanent part of their daily lifestyle.

Peter not only accepted God's forgiveness, but eventually forgave himself. The level of his boldness and commitment to the gospel has rarely been duplicated throughout history. His resolution was so complete that when the Romans sought to crucify him, he would not allow them to hang him upright on the cross in the manner that Jesus was crucified.

Self-Blame

During my time of despair, God was working on my behalf to encourage me. One day we received a phone call from David Wilkerson, the author of the book, *The Cross and the Switchblade*. I was not home at the time and he spoke to Virginia, asking her to give me this message. "Your husband is a good man," he said. "He committed adultery, but he is not an adulterer. This is not a reflection of his lifestyle." David Wilkerson's words challenged me to become more persistent than ever in my prayer life to discover why I had fallen into such a shameful sin.

As you go through the healing process, you will react in a variety of ways. For example, because I was not able to forgive myself at the time of my exposure, I assumed full responsibility for all the fallout around me. When I saw my wife discouraged and unconcerned about the household chores, I blamed myself for her depression.

Self-blame carried over toward my children. Their struggles, financial woes, and the rejection they suffered added greatly to my pain. I watched the church that I had formerly pastored as it began to shatter and members scattered. I wept with feelings of anger, remorse, shame, resentment, and bitterness. For all these things I continually blamed myself.

Several years ago I was counseling with a young man who had made some poor financial investments. This situation created a severe strain on his family. To complicate matters, his father, brother, and brother-in-law verbally attacked him for his unwise decisions. I counseled with him for a period of several months and for a time he seemed to be making progress. Unfortunately, he continued to receive criticism from certain family members.

During a visit to the place he was staying while taking special therapy for his depression, I prayed with him and once more urged him to keep a positive outlook, knowing that God truly loved him. As I left the room I could sense his lack of self-esteem was continuing to erode. Even though we had talked about his beautiful family and how much his wife and children loved him, it seemed I could not help him break the bondage of depression. He continually expressed, "I just can't pray anymore."

Early the next morning I received a phone call. The man had placed the barrel of a 12-gauge shotgun under his chin, pulled the trigger, and killed himself. He died because he could not find a way to forgive himself.

Why have I shared a story with such a tragic outcome? It taught me how far severe depression and the lack of self-worth can drive a person.

Who Is My Accuser?

Before and after my sin became public, I cried out to God for forgiveness. After leaving my pulpit at First Assembly, arrangements were made for me to occupy an office at our television studios. This was my place of solitude to seek God for answers. I continued to ask, "Why? Why? Why?"

Slanderous accusations constantly bombarded me. The criticism caused a spirit of condemnation to hover over me. One day at the studio, after a prolonged season of prayer, the Lord asked me, "Son, what do you want Me to forgive you for?"

I felt confused and said, "Lord, You know all the things they are accusing me of. I know that years ago You forgave me of the sin I committed."

Suddenly, I understood what the Lord was endeavoring to communicate to my spirit. These people were not qualified to be my accusers. Only *He* was!

The Lord spoke to me again: "Do you remember pulling into the parking garage, walking up the stairway to your office, and passing the little lady who handed you an envelope every Sunday morning?" This lady would simply state, "Pastor, here's your coffee money for this week." Inside that envelope were always 15 worn dollar bills.

The Lord continued: "Do you remember that a member of your church sent a tailor to your office and had you fitted with the finest suits? Do you remember when you dined at restaurants, and the waiter said, 'Pastor, don't bother paying for the meal. Someone picked up your ticket.' "

I defensively replied, "Well, Lord, I never asked them to do that."

He countered: "No, you didn't ask for those things, but you thought you deserved them. You didn't merit any of it. *I gave it to you!*"

I recognized that the rebuke I was receiving from the Lord was because I had allowed pride to creep into my life and subtly undermine me. His words echoed again in my mind and I cried because of the pride in my heart. "Oh, God, forgive me!"

Instead of being humiliated by the Lord's message, I was relieved. Suddenly, I felt His loving hands upon me. He removed the burning pain that I had been feeling from the merciless attacks of my accusers.

Unfortunately, much of the anguish we suffered during the process of restoration was inflicted by individuals who took it upon themselves to be God's instrument of correction. The Lord helped me to understand this when He revealed to my heart one day: "The apostle Paul would never admit that he was a prisoner of Rome."

I responded, "But he was."

As the thought "he was not a prisoner of Rome" challenged me, I opened my Bible and read, "Paul, a prisoner of Jesus Christ..." (Philem. 1). The Spirit again spoke: "Don't ever say men put you where you are. I have allowed these circumstances so that I may mold your life for My purpose."

True repentance became a reality when I thoroughly understood and accepted the responsibility for my own actions and stopped pointing an accusing finger at others. It was a point I had to reach before healing could come to the recesses of my soul. Finally, that wonderful day arrived when I released the entire matter to Him. Not only did I accept God's forgiveness, but I totally and completely forgave myself. It was the dawn of a brand-new day.

Chapter 14

Seven Steps to Restoration

"We know he has a reputation for being a thief, but we believe we can help him," a young couple in my church told me.

They were talking about Mike, a 12-year-old boy they had witnessed to about Christ and brought to our church. On the surface, his problem appeared to be a lack of honesty. He had been suspended from school and was headed for serious trouble with the law. We soon realized, however, that his difficulties ran much deeper.

He was constantly beaten by his drunken mother. After intensive efforts at restoration, the couple in our church took the boy into their home and accepted him as their own son.

Mike had a genuine born-again spiritual experience that transformed his life. At the same school where he had caused so much trouble, he became an honor roll student and won the city championship in track. At his high school graduation, the principal lauded him for being a role model for other students. Mike is now attending college and is a strong witness for Christ.

During the past several decades of ministry, I have seen God bring inner healing to people of all ages, all races, and all social backgrounds. After finding answers for my own life, there are proven principles I can now share with others. Here are seven specific steps in the process of restoration.

1. Identify the problems.

I wish I could tell you there is a quick fix for the issues that trouble your life. Yes, salvation takes place in a moment's time and you can instantly become a child of God. Repentance, however, is often a long-term process because of the time it may take to uncover the true causes of problems.

God reveals our innermost problems in a variety of ways, such as through prayer, through reading the Word, through a prophet of God, or as a result of biblical counseling.

I am a strong believer in Christian counseling, but there are three guidelines you should use when choosing a person or a group of people to help you work through your crisis:

A. Find a person who is spiritually mature enough to tell you, "I heard God's voice."

B. Avoid counseling with your best friend, who might be prone to whitewash the issue and tell you that you really have no problem at all.

C. Do not confess your faults to someone who is prone to gossip.

When you find a person who meets these three criteria and you submit yourself to God's restorative plan, divine revelation will begin to operate.

One Sunday night at the end of my sermon, a young mother whom I had never seen responded to the invitation. Standing on either side of her, clinging to her dress, were two beautiful, blonde, five-year-old twin girls. After praying for her, the Spirit spoke to me, "Ask her what is the problem with the two children."

The woman broke into sobs, her body shaking as she slumped to the floor on her knees. She told me, "I work full time to help support our family. My husband works on an off-shore oil rig; he works seven days and is home seven days. When he is home, he takes care of our twins to save on baby-sitting expenses." The woman buried her head in her hands as she told me, "Yesterday, I discovered my husband has been molesting our two little daughters while I was at work."

I began counseling the woman. My advice was that she needed to report the husband, which she did.

Unfortunately, their marriage was not salvageable. The inner healing process was only beginning for the mother and her daughters. The mother had to work through feelings of self-blame, anger, and hate. She finally reached a place of forgiveness and realized that judgment is solely in the hands of God.

The scars of molestation are deep. But the good news is that the blood of Christ covers all sin, both what we have committed and what has been committed against us. I continue to pray for those young girls. It has been my experience that children respond quickly to the healing process when the events are brought into the open and they ask the Lord to remove the stain of sin.

2. Seek forgiveness for the problems you identify.

This is a process which includes the following:

A. *Call on God.* Find a place to pray that is private so you can speak frankly to the Lord without the fear of others hearing. Pray in an open and honest manner and completely unburden your heart to Him.

B. *Repent.* Remember, repentance is not a one-time event, but should be an on-going part of your Christian experience. Approach the process with joy and repent *daily* to the Lord.

If you have sinned against a spouse, don't be tempted to fall into the old trap of saying, "But I already said

I was sorry." Each request for forgiveness deepens and solidifies the healing process. One day you will know in your heart that forgiveness is complete. Then "I'm sorry" will no longer be necessary.

Each time you repent, you chip away at the source of the difficulty, slowly removing layer after layer of hindrances. It will result in a restored relationship between you, God, and those you may have harmed.

   C. *Forgive yourself.* The real ability to forgive yourself lies in understanding that God forgives you and accepts you completely. As you pray daily and confess His forgiveness openly, you will notice a marked change in self-awareness. You will come to know who you are in Christ.

Memorize Scriptures that reassure you of God's forgiveness and of His unwavering love for you as a person. Then quote them aloud when you pray. The Bible tells us, "For with the heart man believeth unto righteousness; and with the mouth confession is made unto salvation" (Rom. 10:10).

Never hesitate to speak audibly about how much God loves you. The Word of God strongly teaches that your mouth is the rudder of the whole body. The direction your words take is the course your body will follow.

Your words are powerful. They are important keys to unlocking the doors of forgiveness.

3. Bury the problems of your past.

People who face a current crisis often find they are dealing with issues they thought were handled years earlier. In reality, those deep issues are the foundation of the current situation.

Friend, you need to have a burial service for the injuries and mistakes of your past. Give them a permanent farewell and turn them completely over to the Lord. If He no longer remembers them, why should you allow the situation to torment you?

A member of our congregation brought her cousin to see me. The young woman was suffering from an acute case of fear. I began counseling the woman and her husband. He told me, "When I leave for work, she often has panic attacks. She calls me and I have to rush back to the house. There have been times when the attack was so serious I had to take her to the hospital."

The situation continued for years and the husband missed work so often that he eventually lost his job. As I led the woman and her husband through the process of inner healing, a layer of new problems began to be revealed.

We discovered that her fear of being alone had its origin in an event that occurred when she was a young child. Her mother constantly paid more attention to her older sister than to her. Once she was left by herself on her birthday while her mother spent the day with her sister. The memories of these early experiences were covered with layers of resentment and blame. Over time they had grown into a monster of fear and rejection.

During counseling she realized that the source of her difficulty was the lack of forgiveness toward her mother. When she came to grips with that simple fact, the healing process was greatly accelerated. Her husband now maintains a normal work schedule knowing there is not a potential crisis brewing at home. She truly has been healed.

4. Don't transfer the blame.

One Saturday a man from our church asked me to meet with a friend of his, Bill, who had a drinking problem. He once had been a successful businessman. His wife had left him and his consequent downward spiral left him a hopeless alcoholic. Bill was desperate for help, but didn't want Christianity. He felt his difficulties were caused by his enemies and his current "bad luck." It is normal for individuals whose world is falling apart to seek for another person on whom they can transfer the blame. However, their help can only come as they assume responsibility for the decisions they make.

Bills anger stemmed from his childhood, but his drinking and other bad judgments had only added to it.

When I met him I shared with him God's plan of salvation. Suddenly the Holy Spirit touched his heart and he saw that his torment was not because of others, but because of himself. Yet he still had a hard time believing that God could really change him.

I challenged him to come to church three times a week for six weeks. If he had not changed by then, I told him I wouldn't ask him to return.

To my amazement he was in attendance the next morning. As I prayed for him at the altar, the power of God instantly delivered him from alcoholism. His wife, Gladys, accompanied him to the next service. A few weeks later she was miraculously saved and eventually became an ordained minister.

He later told me, "Preacher, you looked so sincere when you were sharing the gospel with me, I didn't want you to become discouraged trying to reach me. I felt I was a hardened man beyond hope."

Bill and his wife became strong supporters of our ministry.

It is a natural human instinct to transfer blame. It is also self-destructive. There are those who say, "Well, my case is different. The other person really *is* to blame."

Although that may be true, for your own emotional and spiritual healing you must not allow yourself to hold resentment against them. You must forgive completely. Bill's situation never turned around until he stopped blaming others and accepted the blame for what he had done.

How did that principle apply to my own case? Though Jimmy Swaggart caused great pain to me and my family, I could not be healed until I realized that Jimmy was not the real cause for my hurt. *I* had to accept full responsibility.

The moment you attempt to bring someone else into the vortex of your problem, you have confused the issue and covered the underlying cause. We fall into this trap because blame is the easy way of justifying our failures. Remember, it is only when you submit yourself to the mercy of God that you will reach the place where lasting change happens.

5. Allow God to heal the hurt caused to others.

When those we love are harmed by our actions, we experience guilt, self-condemnation, and shame.

My love for my family is so deep that the pain of seeing what I had done to them was almost unbearable. I wish I could say to you that the healing in this area is totally complete. Yet, as I share the events of my life, I realize that although the pain is not as great as it once was, it is still there. I know God has forgiven me, and I have forgiven myself, but I can never undo the harm I have caused those close to me. Only God can bring healing and hope to them.

All my grandchildren experienced embarrassment, shame, and hurt because of my failure. It became necessary for one of my sons to speak to the authorities at the school his children attended, requesting that they refrain from making negative comments about my situation.

One of my young grandsons was discussing with his mother a conversation he had with his teacher about church. She asked, "Does your teacher know who your pastor is?"

"Yes," my grandson replied.

"Does she know he is your grandfather?"

"Yes, ma'am," he said.

Sensing his mother's concerns, he added, "Mother, I am not ashamed of my Papa. I don't believe those things they are saying about him." He knows I sinned. He just doesn't believe the lies people had told.

Oh, how I wish my eight precious grandchildren did not have to share any part of my burden. They, too, have had to learn how to forgive. For me, the issue is not the people who tell untruths or repeat the lies they have heard. The truth is that my sin opened the door.

Our son, Mark, faced great difficulties in attempting to maintain a speaking schedule during the first three years following my fall. In the eyes of some leaders, his sin was that he forgave me and stood with me. The pain he endured was because of my actions. Only God knows the anguish I suffered as I overheard his telephone conversations and saw the look on his face as another cancellation came. Through it all, not only was Mark sustained, but he also became a more compassionate minister of the Word because of what he experienced.

I watched, helplessly, as each of my children suffered.

How did I find healing from the misery I was enduring as a result of hurts I had inflicted on others? *Repentance was the key!*

I repented for my actions.

I repented for allowing myself to agonize over what I could not change.

I repented of the anger that I felt toward myself and for the self-hatred and bitterness that I so often felt.

I repented for the self-righteous attitude I had in thinking that my judgment was better than God's.

I stopped condemning myself. The Lord began to open my understanding to the fact that it was impossible to love myself and to condemn myself at the same time.

I realized I could not love others to a greater extent than I could love myself. Regardless of how much I wanted to love people and minister to them, I had to love myself first. Only then could I demonstrate true compassion and understanding.

6. Confess your problem to God and to others.

Admitting your failures to the Lord is an essential part of the healing process. Confession is not only good for the soul, it is also necessary for spiritual survival. Again and again I tell people, "Don't hesitate to confess your transgression to the Lord several times each day over a period of at least six months." It places the problem exactly where it should be.

What about your confession to others? You need to approach this subject with much prayer and great sensitivity. Truth is necessary, but you do not want to needlessly allow your confession to harm those around you.

Unless the Lord definitely impresses upon you to go to people who may have been hurt by you in times past, just commit it totally to God. Ultimately your sin was against God and Him alone. As the psalmist wrote, "Against Thee, Thee only, have I sinned, and done this evil in Thy sight" (Ps. 51:4a).

I do not agree with those who contend that every person who has been touched by your failure should be told the details of your sin. You should not feel obligated to say anything more than this: "I'm sorry, and I ask you to forgive me."

For it is a shame even to speak of those things which are done of them in secret (Ephesians 5:12).

It is impossible to receive inner healing if one is unwilling to make an open confession of sin before the

Lord in prayer. Your petition must be honest and not self-justifying. Be willing to accept total responsibility.

7. Realize that restoration is a process.

Inner healing is constant and ongoing. It is not only God's way of binding the wounds of your past, but also His way of protecting you from future hurts.

Many Christians do not understand how the blood of Jesus actually works in regard to cleansing us from sin. The Bible expressly states that when we are saved, the blood of Jesus is applied to our lives. His blood not only covers our sins, but its long-lasting effects are like an antibiotic in our spiritual blood system.

I once knew a young man who suffered from leukemia. His disease impaired his body's ability to manufacture the white blood cells that fight off disease. After an extensive search among his relatives, one of his near kin was able to donate bone marrow to him. Through this bone-marrow transplant, he was infused with blood stem cells so that his body could produce mature white cells. The relative's marrow became permanently engrafted into the bone, and for the rest of his life it enabled him to ward off sickness.

This is how the blood of Jesus works in our lives to ward off future failures. His Spirit mingles with your spirit. Then, the next time you are tempted to fall, it will do battle on your behalf to begin the healing process even before a wound occurs. This is the powerful and continuing impact of the blood of Jesus upon your life. It will always be there to battle for your welfare.

Another reason for being involved in a perpetual healing process is that most people have extremely long memories when it comes to the failures of others. During the restoration process, people will confront you with questions you dealt with years ago. Rather than rebuffing them rudely, you must patiently explain once again how the glory of God restored you.

"Why can't people just forgive and forget?" This is a good question, but the answer is not what you suspect. If you handle the situation properly, you will find an opportunity to minister hope and healing to them.

Paul showed us that those who judge you need inner healing themselves. He declared, "Therefore thou art inexcusable, O man, whosoever thou art that judgest: for wherein thou judgest another, thou condemnest thyself; for thou that judgest doest the same things" (Rom. 2:1).

The force behind judgment is often man's own guilty conscience. If people try to bring up your past sins, it is entirely possible they are struggling with the same issue in their own life. Much too often I have seen men who had personal sexual difficulties condemn others in their battle against the same type of problem.

Roy, a minister friend of mine, lacked patience with those he felt didn't have enough faith. Before he was a

Christian, he was a regional sales manager for a national bourbon distillery. After he came to the Lord, he harshly judged anyone who even *thought* of taking medication instead of believing the Lord for healing. I watched many times as this middle-aged man pointed his finger at the audience and said, "If you had faith, you would never get sick."

I thought to myself, *One day, no doubt, the Lord will teach him to be a little more merciful to others.*

One night he was preaching at a neighboring church in our city. Roy's voice thundered throughout the building when he suddenly caught himself in mid-sentence and gasped, holding his side. He slumped to the floor, writhing in pain from an attack of appendicitis. They rushed him to the hospital and performed emergency surgery.

I arrived just as he was coming out of the anesthetic and was thanking the doctor for treating him. When he saw me walk into the room, he turned to me and sheepishly said, "Brother Gorman, it is amazing how one softens his views on healing after he almost dies." Roy and I have since laughed about his previous hardline views.

God has a way of maturing us and shaping our lives for effective ministry.

The Bible teaches that patience is the key to faith. The apostle James emphasized this point when he said,

"...the trying of your faith worketh patience. But let patience have her perfect work, that ye may be perfect and entire, wanting nothing" (Jas. 1:3-4).

Don't give up too soon. No matter how far you may have fallen, God will guide each step you take on the pathway back. Years ago I remember hearing the words of a Southern gospel song:

> "We're on the glory road.
> Heaven is now in view.
> Though it be rough at times,
> Jesus will see us through."

Chapter 15

Standing on the Rock

Several times I have been asked, "Marvin, how did you know that God's seal of approval was once again stamped on your life and it was safe for you to take up spiritual responsibility and authority once more?"

I know that God's plan for each individual is unique, but for me, several things had to happen.

First, I had to realize that my sin was against God, and God alone.

Second, the transgression I committed became revolting to me.

Third, I came to the place where I knew that God's judgment on my life was not unjust, but truly a blessing in disguise.

When those things occurred, a confidence began to build within me that I would once again be trustworthy in my actions. My prayer life began to take on a healthy rhythm. I knew I was standing firm on the Solid Rock.

Many people have wondered why I did not submit to the restoration process that was presented to me by the Assemblies of God denomination. The rehabilitation program involves a commitment where an offending pastor or leader must move to a different city and place himself under another pastor's supervision for a period of two years. The first year he is not allowed to speak from any pulpit. During the second year the reprimanded and reformed individual is then allowed to assist the supervising pastor in whatever capacity he deems necessary. At the end of the second year, the restored leader is once again returned to ministry.

When I requested the church officials to allow me to enter the rehabilitation program, they asked me to confess to allegations that did not occur. It was out of the question for me to admit to lies. Therefore, they declined my request. Please understand, the program established by the Assemblies of God has been extremely helpful in restoring many ministers. Unfortunately, it was something in which I could not participate.

A New Home

God always brings good out of any situation. That's what He did for me as I remained in New Orleans under His direction. God used the accusations like a hammer to chisel away blemishes in my life. The years of restoration have not been easy and often I have been lonely. But in the depths of this healing process, I have developed a relationship with the Lord far beyond my expectations. As God told the prophet Isaiah, "For a small moment have I forsaken thee; but with great mercies will I gather thee" (Is. 54:7).

Fear can blind us from seeing God's willingness to extend mercy and grace, and to eagerly restore everything that satan takes away. For example, soon after I resigned as pastor of First Assembly of God, my total means of financial support was cut off and I was forced to declare bankruptcy. The loss of my home was not only devastating to me, but it also caught the media's eye. *USA Today* printed an article concerning it.

The same day the story hit the national press, I received a call from Bill Swad, a pastor and a Christian businessman in Columbus, Ohio. Bill owns one of the largest Chevrolet dealerships in the United States and is a brother in the Lord. It was refreshing just to hear his faith-filled voice on the phone. "Marvin," he exclaimed, "I read in *USA Today* that you are losing your house. What are you going to do?"

"I suppose we'll have to rent a house," I replied.

"Why don't you buy another one?" he asked.

"Well, you don't understand, Bill," I hesitantly said. "I'm in the middle of bankruptcy and there is no one in the state of Louisiana who will lend me the money to buy a new residence."

"You go find a home and I will finance it." (While we were in Akron, Ohio, for counseling in July, 1986, Bill and his wife, Sally, drove over from Columbus, to see us. They gave our ministry a substantial donation. Now they were once again coming to our rescue.)

"I hardly know what to say," I replied. "My wife did see a home she liked while she was looking for rental property."

"Get an appraisal and find out what you can buy it for." Bill quickly hung up the phone.

The house my wife chose was owned by a local bank, which had foreclosed on a previous owner. The appraisal value was $226,000, but we were told we could have it for $125,000. Bill financed the entire amount! He also loaned us extra money so we could update the air-conditioning system and do other minor repairs on the premises. Because of this totally unexpected miracle, we never found ourselves homeless.

My friend, God never stopped caring for us. Though we were under His corrective hand, He gently provided for us and made sure that we would not fall too hard.

Time for Repair

My mother-in-law, Mimi, used to live in El Dorado, Arkansas. For years she was a professional seamstress for one of the city's largest dry-cleaning establishments. I remember visiting her neatly-organized sewing room and watching as she worked on expensive silk suits worn by prominent businessmen of the town, altering them with her creative hands.

It was a running joke in our family that whenever I bought a new suit, she had to check it out. She would run her fingers down the seams and comment that a particular pocket was not layered correctly, or that the inseam needed to be taken up on the pants. I never felt badly about her criticism, for not only was she proficient in recognizing the fault, she was also very capable of repairing it. It's one thing for a person to criticize in order to help bring correction and healing. It is quite another if someone is doing it because of a self-righteous attitude.

When my mother-in-law commented about one of my suits not fitting correctly, she promptly took the article of clothing to her sewing room and repaired it. Her purpose was to dress her son-in-law like a perfect gentleman.

Don't you see? This is what Jesus does. The reason He points out our faults is because He is the only person in the world who has the ability to rectify them. His purpose is not to humiliate, but to perfect.

The Lord's correction may not seem pleasant at first. At the time of this writing, I have been in the restoration process several years and the effects of the

Master Tailor continue to be manifested. From all over America and various parts of the world, I have received calls from friends who are thrilled with what Jesus is doing in me. I know He will do the same for you.

Lost and Found

Jim was a solid member of First Assembly and had a reputation for no-nonsense Christianity. Before he was converted, he had spent a major part of his life in the French Quarter of New Orleans, snorting coke and constantly drinking alcohol. When God saved him, there was an instant transformation.

About the same time I was defrocked, Jim's life was thrown into a tailspin. After much turmoil, including a divorce, he was bitter, angry, and ready to attack anybody who got in his way. Working in the French Quarter only seemed to deepen his despair.

One day his mind reeled back to his former pastor and he thought about contacting me, but was afraid to make the phone call. When he finally dialed my number, I could sense his hesitation on the phone. We agreed to meet privately at a coffee shop located near a busy highway. With the sound of cars slipping down the highway in the background, Jim quietly poured out his heart to me. "I don't know what you are going to think of me after I tell you this, Brother Gorman, but I am back on alcohol and in deep trouble."

After he made this confession, we both felt a wave of God's mercy and grace. I then began to share with him the same principles that I am explaining in this book. His restoration has not been easy nor quick, but it has been complete. Jim has remarried a beautiful Christian woman and has been very successful in his profession. He is a faithful member of our church.

If restoration was not possible, God would not have put the word in the Bible. To restore something is to bring it back to the original or better condition.

A friend of mine once refurbished an old car. He was able to make it not only new-looking, but actually exceeded the quality of the original model. He installed technological advances to the car that the manufacturer couldn't have accomplished because they weren't available when the car was first made. A person's mistake does not signal the end of his life or ministry. Through the workings of repentance it becomes the refining process that produces restoration for God's divine purpose.

The Verdict

In 1991, after endless court depositions and legal haggling, my lawsuit against Jimmy Swaggart, his ministry, and others came to trial. Since it was in the hands of the bankruptcy trustee, the action was something I could not stop.

For ten weeks we were in that courtroom. The emotional stress was intense. Jimmy and Frances were faced with the statements they and others in their organization had written or spoken about me that returned like a boomerang. Reporters hung on every word.

When the verdict of the jury was read, they agreed that the fall of my ministry was the result of a well-orchestrated conspiracy. We won the highly-publicized case and the judge announced a large monetary award in our favor.

The final settlement, however, was less than the original judgment. I did not receive any of the proceeds. The money was used to pay my creditors from the bankruptcy.

My actions caused the Swaggart family tremendous pain. For this I am truly sorry. Both of our families are fully acquainted with the pain of public embarrassment. Today, God has restored my ministry in New Orleans and given me a thriving congregation at our church, Temple of Praise. He has reestablished our radio and television outreach. Our radio program is aired locally six days each week. We are on a New Orleans television station each Sunday morning, as well as 156 other stations across America.

Recently I ministered to a group of more than 40,000 in Africa, with a standing invitation to return for their conferences. Additional plans are being made to fulfill other invitations on foreign soil.

My wife and I, along with our three children and their families, are continuing to serve the King of kings, and we are giving God all the glory.

Once I stood before the mighty Niagara Falls. The water was crashing down with the sound of fury. Then I looked beyond the torrent and saw a flowing river that was peaceful and calm.

My friend, no matter what you have experienced, there is a bright promise ahead. I can assure you from personal experience and on the authority of God's Word, there is life beyond the fall.

Please visit our website at **www.marvingorman.com** for an overview of our ministry. While at our website we invite you to browse our online bookstore for all of Marvin Gorman's current ministry resources, books, CD's and DVD's.

Foundation For Human Helps
1440 State Hwy 248 Suite Q-167
Branson, MO 65616
417-336-4685